Grief Relief

Practical Prescriptions To Ease Pain and Hurt After Any Significant Loss

By

Stan E. DeKoven, Ph.D.

Stan E. DeKoven, Ph.D.

Grief Relief

Published by:
Vision Publishing
1115 D Street
Ramona, California 92065
www.visionpublishingservices.com

Printed in the United States of America

First printing: January, 1991
Second printing: January, 1995
Third Printing: January, 1996
Fourth Printing: January 1999
Second Edition January 2003
Third Edition October 2006

Stan E. DeKoven, Ph.D.

Table Of Contents

Stan E. DeKoven, Ph.D.

Foreword to this Second Edition

After over 40 years as a pastor and Christian counselor it is abundantly clear to me that there are no answers to any problem without Jesus, and that is why Dr. DeKoven's book is so important -- it combines a day to day solution to the grief experience with the eternal wisdom of God's Word.

I believe this book is a valuable, practical, Christian solution to The "Grief Relief" process for the Body of Christ. It can help you know "what to say" when loved ones you care about are in the grieving process.

This is a fine book to send to a friend or loved one who is experiencing, or struggling with, a serious or difficult loss in their life.

Dr. DeKoven, as a practicing Marriage, Child and Family Therapist, is well qualified to be the author of such a book as this.

Joseph J. Bohac, Ph.D.

Note

Dr. Bohac (Doc to all who knew and loved him) went home to be with the Lord on the 9th of December 1999. I will always love and miss my dear friend and co-laborer for Christ, whose influence continues to live on even today.

Stan E. DeKoven, Ph.D.

Forward to the First Edition

Every Christian man or woman will meet grief many times along the path of life - because grief comes in several forms.

We mourn for our lost loved ones, we "feel bad" (a form of mourning) when we move away from old friends; we "hurt" when we lose an important job; we feel "devastated" in a divorce that can rip apart families and cause tremendous economic and psychological adjustments in lifestyle.

All of these emotions are variations on grief we will inevitably experience sometime in this life.

Dr. Stan DeKoven, a practicing family counselor in San Diego, has helped literally hundreds of patients work through the grief process. He has developed several key steps from Scripture that are practical ways to overcome and shorten the time you, your loved ones or friends, spend grieving.

I believe this book is a valuable, practical, Christian solution to the "grief relief" process for the Body of Christ.

It can help you to know "what to say" when loved ones that you care about are in the grieving process.

You may even want to consider giving this book to a friend or loved one you know is struggling today with a serious loss in their life.

After thirty years as President and Founder of the Full Gospel Business Men's Fellowship, it is abundantly clear to me that there are no answers to any problem without Jesus, and that is why Dr.

Stan's book is so important - it combines a day to day solution to the grief experience with the eternal wisdom of God's Word.

May this book abundantly bless you and your loved ones.

Demos Shakarian
Founder/President
Full Gospel Business Men's
Fellowship International

Special Acknowledgments

I deeply appreciate the Church of the Lord Jesus Christ -- it is alive, vibrant, and powerfully able to give care and comfort to those in need.

A special thanks to Reverend Edward Feezell for his excellent research on an original manuscript, and to Mr. Mike Wourms, Christian Services Network, the staff of Vision Publishing, and Vision International University.

A hearty "thank you" also goes to the precious families who have shown me tremendous courage in the face of their own personal grief.

Acknowledgements to the Third Edition

I am grateful to the Lord for His power to reconcile and restore all who have suffered the loss of a loved one. To you, I say, "His grace is sufficient!"

Dedication

This book is dedicated to Karen S. DeKoven, Carma Louise DeKoven, Jack Frates, Dr. Joe Bohac and Dr. Doug Jarrard. You are loved and missed; we honor you.

Stan E. DeKoven, Ph.D.

Introduction

"Courage is not the absence of fear and pain, but the affirmation of life despite fear and pain"
Rabbi Earl Grollman

The sense of shock and bewilderment was overwhelming. Cynthia's* husband, a successful and beloved man of God, had died of cancer after a long illness. The normal feelings of sadness and hurt were mixed with an awesome awareness of God's presence.

The first few days after the memorial service Cynthia was on auto pilot. As per her personality, she focused on making sure everyone else was cared for...her nearly grown children, her church family, even friends. Having served as a lay leader in her church, the role of care giver was both comfortable and functional.

It took several days, leading to weeks, before the full realization of her loss came, and with it the pain, grief, and mourning. Her plans, purposes, dreams, and hopes had to be reassessed. Finances were tight, decisions on the future had to be made, and the realization that excepting her family, she was alone, became only too painfully clear. Grief and loss were being experienced in full force. Her only course was to manage life, day by day, with the comfort of the Holy Spirit. The future was unknown, but with courage, Cynthia, like thousands of others, would make it. But what would the future hold?

* The names and events have been altered for privacy, though the story is true.

13

"We have the power either of withstanding the spring, and sinking back into the cosmic winter, or of going on...It remains with us...To die in this winter, or to go on into that spring and that summer" C.S. Lewis.

MOURNING IN AMERICAN CULTURE

Part of the difficulty when grieving is that our American culture no longer validates our status as a griever. There are few helps or symbols (such as a black armband) to acknowledge that you are grieving beyond the funeral. Society has taught us that overt displays of grief are not acceptable past a week or two of death. You may feel pressure to behave "normally" and "to produce" as if nothing has changed in your life.

People continue to receive messages from their family, friends and employers to "get a grip", "get on with life", and "it's time to get over this" as soon as two or three weeks after a death of a loved one. Americans haven't learned that people aren't having emotional breakdowns just because they aren't showing overt symptoms of grief.

Many other cultures are far more realistic about how long mourning requires. Many have the custom of dressing in black up to six months or a year. It is the Orthodox Jewish custom to offer formal prayers daily for 11 Hebrew months and to mourn for 12 months.

If you would like to give your family, friends, and employers something that explains your grieving behavior, consider using this letter.

My dear (Family, Friends, Pastor, Employer...)

As you know I have recently experienced the death of my (   ).

This loss is devastating to me and it will take time for me to work through my grief. Sometimes I fear that you may expect me to heal quickly, but grief can not be rushed.

I will cry more often than usual for a while. My tears symbolize the release of my feelings and are a healthy sign that I am recovering. These tears are neither a sign of personal weakness nor a lack of faith or hope.

Because my emotions are all heightened by the strain of grief, I may seem irrational at times. Please be patient and forgiving, if I become irritable and angry for no apparent reason. Grief comes in unpredictable ways.

I know that you are probably at a loss for what to do or say to help me. There are no magic words you can say to take my pain away. Touch me or give me a hug to let me know you care.

Please don't wait for me to call you. I am often too overwhelmed to think of reaching out for help. I need you more than ever in the months ahead, but my pride sometimes prevents me from telling you. Give me space to heal, but don't allow me to withdraw from you.

Pray for me, if you wish; but pray that I will find the courage and the strength I need to deal with my grief constructively. Faith is not an excuse from the process of grief.

If by chance you have had a similar loss, please share it with me. It will not make me feel worse. Grief shared is grief diminished.

Telling me to "Cheer up, it could be worse" makes me feel discounted and angry. This loss is the worst thing for me right now. But I will heal and live again. While there are still painful days ahead for me I will not always feel as I do now. One day I will be able to laugh again and find new joy in living.

I appreciate your concern and caring. Your under-standing and support is a gift which I will always treasure.

Sincerely,

"The main thing in life is not to be afraid to be human"

Pablo Casals

Loss is Tough!

Just think for a moment how upset you get when you "lose" your car keys or your wallet. Your blood pressure goes up. Your voice gets shrill. You start to shout at anything that moves.

Normally you are a patient human being, but the loss of your car keys instantly transforms you into an irascible tiger ready to bite off the head of the first person crazy enough to try to talk to you.

Maybe the car keys example is a bit melodramatic; but not by much. The plain fact is most of us cannot handle even the simple loss of a rather insignificant possession.

Now, if the loss of a wallet or a set of car keys can trigger emotional reactions that affect both your mind and your body --how much more will the loss of someone or something infinitely more significant -- such as the loss of a loved one (through death or divorce) -- or the loss of a home, the loss of a child (through death or moving out) -- cause us to experience a myriad set of roller-coaster emotions?

Loss is traumatic. Loss hurts. And the separation pains of loss take time to heal.

Loss and separation are related terms that describe a universal phenomena experienced by everyone. The many different kinds of separation may be classified into two general types: developmental and situational.

Developmental separations are an inherent part of the growth stages that human beings experience from birth through death. Separation is the natural result of the ever changing stages of human development throughout the life span of each individual. Any kind of separation can cause anxiety and concern. Certain types of separation can be much more traumatic. Frequently, separations are a part of the natural passage from one psychosocial stage to another (Erikson, 1968).

Some separations are predictable. They may not be as unsettling as those that are less predictable, such as separations resulting from an accident, a rape, birth of a deformed child, or a geographic move, etc. Even separation from a hope, an interest or a physical symptom can be a traumatic loss.

One of the most difficult realities that pastors, counselors, or any effective community and church leader will invariably face in their service to families is; how to comfort those who have lost someone they love, or who have experienced other significant losses -- such as job, home, or spouse (through death or divorce).

The "empty nest" syndrome is experienced by many mothers when the last child has left home. One must also consider the loss of separation experienced by many children when they leave home. Bolby (1969) saw what he believed was a universal and specific syndrome of reactions to separation and loss in his studies on the separation of children from their parents. In his studies he identifies three stages --

protest, despair, and detachment -- as essentially the same for all separations.

A common element of separation is stress. Kubler-Ross (1969) and others have delineated the stages of grief and loss in relation to the loss experienced by the death of a loved one. The stages that Ross described are: <u>denial</u>, <u>anger</u>, <u>bargaining</u>, <u>depression</u> and <u>acceptance</u>. When a person is permitted to and even assisted in experiencing and resolving these various stages through a broadly defined time span, healing and restoration can occur. These will be discussed later in this book.

Different States for Different Folks

Many different things determine how an individual reacts to separation and loss, they include: 1) the nature of the person experiencing the separation; 2) the nature or quality and quantity of the loss involved in the separation; 3) the nature of the milieu in which the separation occurs (Mahler, 1975).

In the case of significant separation through loss, the cognitive and emotional process of working through that significant loss is called **grief.** Grieving, although painful, can and should be viewed as a healthy response. Without it a complete emotional recovery is not possible.

When the grieving process is not accomplished within a certain time limit, it may develop into what would be classified as **abnormal grieving.** Abnormal grief may occur immediately following a loss resulting in a psychotic reaction in which the individual is totally unable to cope. Another reaction is when the pain of the loss is completely disowned and the individual proceeds with a "life as usual" attitude, as if nothing has happened.

Another abnormal reaction has been called the "shrine" syndrome, which is symbolic of the survivor's inability to let go of their loved one. When the symptoms of grief are not substantially resolved within eighteen months[1], professional help is indicated. Most Americans carry a strong Judeo-Christian belief system. As Christians, we know in our hearts, that death is only the instantaneous transition from this life to the next. Yet, even though we know this through head knowledge, and may even believe it deep within our hearts -- there still remains a necessary and normal God-given grief process that each person must be allowed to experience in their own time and in their own unique way.

Saying good-bye to a loved one who has died is never easy. Knowing that the person "is now in heaven" helps, but that knowledge, for most, is not enough to take away the sting and pain of separation.

That separation pain is not limited to the experience of the death of a loved one. Separation from a safe and secure job is often as shocking and painful as becoming separated from an arm or a leg. Physicians tell us that it is not uncommon for a person with a severed limb to actually "feel" the limb for several months as though it were still attached. The body

---

[1] This is only a guideline. To a certain extent we may never recover to the place of forgetting. Further, many losses, especially that of a child, can take and needs to take significantly longer to process through.

refuses to let go of that already severed limb. This affect was noted as long ago as the early 1930's in what Freud later called the phantom response by Simmel (1966).

This term described a delusional perception of the presence of any body part subsequent to it's removal or loss (Simmel, 1966). Still, families and friends become worried that "mother has lost her grip on reality" if she forgetfully refers to her husband as though he were still living for a few months immediately following his death, or a husband dresses to go to work even though he was fired a week ago!

Separation recovery takes time. There is a necessary adjustment period, and that period of adjustment applies to other losses besides death.

When a family is jolted through a divorce or other significant separation, adults and children both go through a traumatic time. The fact that the separation may not last an extended period of time, such as when a military parent is sent to a military operation for an indeterminate time, does not eliminate the anguish. The pain of separation is just as great. The daddy who was always around to fix the wagon, take out the garbage, or mend the fence is now gone. It takes time to get over the reality of separation, and separation almost always hurts.

Every loss we face in our lives prepares us for our death and the final transition into eternal fellowship with God. Even though we know this truth, the preparation can still be painful. However, through each dramatic transition, we can rest in the knowledge that we have a Comforter who walks with us.

> *Even though I walk through the valley of the shadow of death, I fear no evil; for Thou art with me; Thy rod and Thy staff, they comfort me* (Psalms 23:4 NASB).

Significant life transitions or transitions of any kind are an opportunity for pastors, psychologists, counselors and lay-leaders to help hurting people fully experience grief relief and enter into a process which leads to comfort and victory.

> *Cast your burden upon the LORD, and He will sustain you; He will never allow the righteous to be shaken* (Psalms 55:22 NASB).

This book has been specifically written to help the counselor, pastor, lay-leader minister, and the hurting person to:

1. Recognize the Grief Relief process,
2. Accept it as normal, and then
3. Learn how to work through that process with the transforming and sustaining power of Jesus Christ.

I pray that the tools of ministry which God has given to me in my counseling practice, will help each person reading this book learn how to reduce the trauma of loss in their life, and increase the thrill of their Christ-centered walk.

For all things are for your sakes, so that the grace which is spreading to more and more people may cause the giving of thanks to abound to the glory of God.

Therefore we do not lose heart, but though our outer man is decaying, yet our inner man is being renewed day by day (2 Cor 4:15-16 NASB).

Stan E. DeKoven, Ph.D.

Chapter One

Grief Relief - A Common Cry

The LORD is near to the brokenhearted, And saves those who are crushed in spirit. (Psalms 34:18 NASB).

I was in the Army, stationed at Fort Leonard Wood (we called it "Lost in the Woods"), Missouri when I received the call that my Grandpa Ralph had passed away. Ralph was actually my step-grandfather on my dad's side of the family, but really the only grandfather I had known.

Ralph Dean (a cousin to Dizzy Dean the Hall of Fame baseball player) could present himself as a grizzly, surly old man, yet he was always an encouragement to me with regards to my baseball career. I am sure he was somewhat disappointed when I decided on graduate school instead of giving pro-ball a shot (a distant one, I think) yet he never showed his disappointment.

I always loved and respected my grandpa. He was so very special, and I experienced a true sense of loss over his death, even disappointment that this special man was gone. I grieved. I hurt in the same way that we all do at the loss of a loved one.

Grief is an emotional and physical reaction to a significant personal loss. We usually think of grief only in relation to the death of a loved one since this is probably the most painful kind of grief.

There are however, really three primary areas of loss that can occur in the lives of most people -- even when a death has not occurred -- and all three areas trigger the need for the God-given grief relief process. These three areas of pain can all be effectively comforted by using the same grief relief principles that I discuss and recommend in dealing with death and grief in this book.

The first area I want to discuss is perhaps the most traumatic.

The Loss Of Relationships

The Lord has designed us as relational human beings. In Genesis 2:18 the Bible says that *it is not good for man to be alone*. Phone counseling services know that the most common need expressed by people of all types is that they "are lonely and just wanted to call and talk to someone."

God created man and woman for fellowship, both with Himself and with one another. Companionship and fellowship are universal needs placed within us by God. When God created Adam, He immediately gave him Eve for companionship. So it is only natural that when we are faced with the possibility of the loss of a significant love relationship, we experience anxiety and fear. When this anxiety and fear of loss comes upon us, we experience pain.

I think you will be amazed at how many different experiences people have that trigger the grief process.

In this area of relationship, I would like to deal mainly with some of the major types of personal loss.

The Loss Of A Friend

Flo, was for many years, my beautiful wife's (Karen) best friend. They met through church and have walked through many interesting and intimate situations together. Even though their basic personalities and backgrounds are extremely different, they bonded into a very close relationship.

When Flo announced that her husband was being transferred (he was in the Navy) to the Chicago area, Karen experienced many of the symptoms of grief which will be looked at later. It was a very difficult time for my wife, and though their relationship continued (much more expensive in phone calls and an annual visit to Chicago), the grief and mourning of the loss was an inevitable process that had to be worked through.

Friendships take time and effort to develop. One person might put in hours upon hours of bowling, Bible study, barbecues and boat outings with his or her friend -- and all of those experiences combine to fulfill the vital need for social contact.

Friends are a very powerful and important influence in our lives. When you lose a friend, whether by death or some other form of separation, such as through moving, it can become a painful experience.

Frankly, most of us do not do a very good job of saying good-bye when we leave a friend. Normally, we try to protect ourselves from the anxiety of such a loss through denial by thinking, "It is not like we are going to be worlds apart," or "You never know, maybe we won't really move," or even through negative projection -- "I never really liked them that much anyway."

Many of us try to avoid saying good-bye, or deal with it tearfully, or even aggressively. In some cases, friends will even start a fight before separating to help ease the pain of departure! The friends usually are not aware that they are subconsciously trying to ease the pain through a fight (it is easier to leave someone who you do not like), but if you think about it for a moment, there was probably a time in your life when you ended a friendship precisely this way.

Fighting, vigorous denial, and negative projection are all safety mechanisms we develop to try to hide the pain. So, what can you do?

To ease the pain of separation, one good practice is to go through the grief relief process, a "rehearsal" if you will, where you actually practice saying good-bye to those who are important to you. Other transitional keys to saying good-bye are discussed later in this book.

Separation Of Husband And Wives

Many times, especially in the lives of military families, as well as for business executives, there are temporary assignment separations between a husband and a wife.

Often, in the good-bye process, where one might expect tenderness and love, there is instead tenseness -- even fighting, just as when friends separate.

Frequently at the reunions, fighting once again occurs. As you can well imagine, in the military, and in businesses that require frequent trips -- this type of behavior can easily put a significant strain on the marriage and family.

These transition periods are very difficult for most couples. Why? Because, hard as it may be to accept, they have never learned how to say "good-bye" and "hello" properly. The anxiety in these periods can be greatly reduced through an understanding of what is taking place in the subconscious mind.

The "good-bye" is an action that triggers the grief process (since it acknowledges that loss is about to take place). By indulging in senseless fighting, it somehow softens the pain of the separation. After all, is it not easier and less painful to say good-bye to someone you are angry with than to say good-bye to someone about whom you care deeply and intimately? It is -- until you master the art of saying good-bye.

I encourage couples to talk openly about their behavior during separation and to work through their fears of not seeing one another again. I also encourage them to develop methods other than fighting to soften the times apart. The following is an example of how this system works.

One wife of a business executive I know always packs in her husband's luggage (every time in a different, secret place) a fuzzy little toy bear. When this couple kisses good-bye there is a sort of childish giggle in their hearts, since both the husband and wife know that soon hubby will "discover" the hidden bear when he arrives at his hotel room. Sharing this mutual "secret" makes the departure easier.

When the executive discovers the bear upon arrival at his destination, he puts it on top of the hotel television in his room. Every time he looks at it, he is reminded how much his wife cares, and this little act of love keeps them close, even during the separation. When the executive arrives back home, the first thing he unpacks is his toy bear, and it goes back up on the bedroom dresser until the next voyage.

I remember the first few times that my wife and I separated. It was not because of any family problems but because of the U.S. Army (and then later, because of business trips and seminars). Each time we prepared to say good-bye to one another, we would first get very tense and anxious, often have an argument, and usually part in a huff.

Later, I would think about it, worry about it, and I would have to ask the Lord to forgive me. My wife would do the same. Then one of us would call the other and try to "make up." But, it was always a problem. We also found that when we were reunited, we often started off again with a fight, even though we vowed not to.

I began reading about and researching the subject of parting. One of the things that I discovered was that we are not alone in this very difficult ritual, like so many, we had never learned how to say hello or good-bye properly.

It is truth that action absorbs anxiety. When we express our feelings with action, the anxiety (fear, insecurity) is momentarily removed. How much better to become aware of this subconscious process, and choose positive methods for transitions. We realized we could skip the arguing part and go right to the making up, which is a lot more fun and much more productive.

With practice any couple can learn to say good-bye, and do so with the open expression of feelings and with a sense of touch and affection. Couples will need to work through the fears and beliefs that this may be the last time of seeing one another. We must recognize that saying good-bye -- and later saying hello --is a very important part of any modern-day relationship.

Loss of Children

When we lose our children -- not through death, but when it is time for them to say "good-bye" and move out on their own -- it may be a painful process for both the parents and the children.

In counseling, psychologists often discover the "empty nest" syndrome in middle-aged mothers. It is called the empty nest because when the mother finds her "baby chicks" gone, she feels her life as a woman no longer has purpose. This is especially true if the wife has made the children the central focus of her life, placing them above the husband in her scheme of priorities. This time of transition begins when the last child finally leaves home.

Mothers often assume that with the loss of their last child, they are no longer a "real" mother to their children. Amazing as it might seem, the same "empty nest" syndrome can affect men as well!

This syndrome can cause a real identity crisis, since the mother no longer feels useful. The role of mother has been so all consuming that the transition period back to the role of "just being a wife" often produces extreme anxiety.

In counseling, I try to gently remind the "empty nest" mother that children are given to us by God for a purpose, and our goal is to raise our children so that we can then release them again to the Lord as adults. At that time of release, we are no longer responsible for their actions. Although we naturally still continue to love and care about our children, we no longer need to bear the burden of their care.

The letting go or separation process begins developmentally in children soon after birth and continues throughout their life with the process being complete by the age of eighteen to twenty-one. However, parents who were not able to resolve the separation anxiety that they experienced as children with their parents will most likely have the greatest amount of difficulty in dealing with separation issues relating to their own children. This would be especially true of adults who were abandoned as children.

Parents must learn to accept the fact that they are going to lose their children. When children become adults and move on to accept the roles of adulthood, they are no longer that little "bundle of joy" that they were. They are now ready to accept the roles of men and women who are serving God and perhaps beginning a family of their own. This does not change the fact that it is difficult to let go of them emotionally.

The process of saying "good-bye" to children must be dealt with, since there will be a time when all children must become adults. Parents must recognize there will be some sadness and hurt, but after the process of grieving, our children are set free to become mature, responsible adults and to pursue their destiny.

The process of saying "good-bye" to children is one that needs to be dealt with consciously. I believe that dealing with the process should be a part of the family planning and talked about openly and often with the children. Our children's freedoms and responsibilities we've tied together with future goals in mind. The ultimate goal I have as a parent is to bring our children into the realm of fully functioning adults.

For example, children are "free" to date if they display the responsibility of getting home on time and staying out of trouble. They are "free" to play after school as long as they exercise the responsibility of getting all of their homework done before it is due.

Divorce

Divorce has lost most of its stigma in our society as a whole as well as in the church. When I was a youth, a divorced woman was always talked about in "loose and easy" terms, and a divorced man could never run for political office. Today, all that has changed.

Unfortunately, divorce occurs in families of all types of people, and in all areas of life, including Christian homes (statistically, it has been shown that divorce occurs in Christian families about as often as it does within the rest of society). Also, divorce occurs as frequently with couples who marry after living together to "see how it goes" for a year or so before marriage, as it does for those couples who do not live together before marriage. We now absolutely know that living together is no predictor of how the marriage will survive.

Divorce is a lot like death -- except that the corpse is still walking around! It is a very painful time for people to go through.

There is probably nothing more damaging to our society, and to the institution of the family, than divorce. However, it is not my intent to fully discuss the dynamics of divorce here, but I do want you to understand that divorce does occur, and that when it does, the same grief process occurs as in a death, and the process must be endured and conquered.

Anger and bitterness surface before, during and after a divorce.

You must learn how to say "good-bye" to a spouse who was once loved, and when you are able to finally do so, freedom results. The pain of a marital breakup is so strong and devastating that it often takes between eighteen months and two years for people to really let go of the loss. In some rare instances, the process may take even longer.

If a complete and total good-bye never comes ("that's it -- it's over -- I've got to get on with my life"), then the potential of repeating the pattern of the past marriage problems emerges in any subsequent relationship. This tragic cycle of broken relationships may continue until a person faces the problems that were inherent in the old relationship -- deals with them -- forgives the offender -- and moves on with their own life. It is difficult to face our own possible or partial responsibility for a divorce, but an honest, open, self-evaluation is essential in "working through" our loss.

In most cases, there is no greater sense of loss than in divorce or death. This statement often bares repeating. Both death and divorce create a sense of sudden abandonment, and both leave feelings of bitterness and anger. It is vital that these feelings be shared so that the Grief Relief process may occur. In the case of a long-term, destructive divorce, or a long-term, painful illness, the pain and agony can be of a much greater intensity and longer lasting.

Separation From Animals

It may seem a little frivolous to discuss the problems of separation from our animals after talking about

37

divorce and separation by death of a loved one, but to many individuals, animals are a very important part of their lives. As human beings, we can become attached to those precious creatures that love us, especially if they respond through barking or purring when we show our affection to them.

The loss of an animal that has met our needs for many years, such as a good dog that has become a loving, constant companion, can result in a sense of hurt and loss -- whether you are a child or an adult. Such a loss can result in a temporary depression, with tears and hurting for the lost and faithful friend.

Counselors have found that animals or pets are a special gift to mankind. They enhance our sense of being worthwhile, they can be a comfort, especially to the very young or old.

I remember so well the loss of my dog, Ginger. I was very young, and Ginger was very special to me as well as to my father. Almost all animal lovers feel that their pet is very special to them. Ginger was a loving, caring mixture of German Shepherd and Collie. She used to sleep at the foot of my bed at night, and would wait for me to come home from school every day. What a faithful friend she was!

We were constant companions. Two or three years after I left home to go into the army, I remember getting that fateful call from home saying that my dog, Ginger had died.

What a tremendous sense of loss and hurt I experienced! I loved that animal. She had been a constant loving and sharing companion for many years. Somehow, I felt that I could talk to my dog even when I could not talk to my friends -- she always seemed to listen and care.

I found myself experiencing a brief but profound depression for a short period of time. I cried, I hurt all because of the loss of an animal that I had truly loved. To lose an animal is a difficult and painful experience, and it is perfectly natural for us to grieve the loss of a pet just as we may grieve over the loss of other relationships.

When loss occurs, a reaction is inevitable. Everyone reacts differently and in varying degrees. How people react can be somewhat predicted in that we all typically will follow the patterns we have learned from our families and within our culture. Yet, in spite of similarities, we are all unique individuals. When a loss occurs we need to be sensitive to one another and learn to be an agent of healing with God's help.

Stan E. DeKoven, Ph.D.

Chapter Two

Loss Of Significant Situations

The grief process is not only triggered by the loss of human and animal relationships. There are many losses of "significant situations" in our lives that trigger the same grief process, and for which the grief relief principle must be applied.

In an article in Grief Work, The Journal of the American Association of Grief Counselors, Inc., Dr. Don C. Coombs (1995) states, "Non-death loses are considered extremely significant in life." He summarized that 50% of those (people) experiencing a non-death loss considered it as significant as a death. The symptoms they experienced were similar to the symptoms of someone experiencing the loss from death. Let me give an example.

Jim was a thirty-eight-year-old man with great ambitions. He had put most of his energy and most of his life savings into a business project he was positive was a "sure thing." Jim had cashed out of his retirement plan early, said good-bye to his old secure job, and decided to "go for it" on his own.

Unfortunately, due to fluctuating market problems and some poor timing, the project faltered. During a five-month period, he struggled with all his might to keep his business afloat. In the end, he lost everything, including his sense of worth and self-esteem. So great was his loss that for several months he was incapacitated, unable to even look for work.

Jim's story is true, and his depressive reactions were fairly typical of someone who experiences the loss of something significant in their life -- including a business or the dream to build a business. Why?

So much of Jim's identity was wrapped up in his work. When his business failed, he felt useless, much like the mother who experiences the "empty nest" syndrome when the last child moves out of the home. When the work ended, so did Jim's sense of purpose which led to the beginning of his depression.

The same syndrome often occurs when men enter into retirement living. Many feel that retirement means that they are no longer useful or that they have been "put out to pasture." Statistically, the most vulnerable time for sudden death in males is within one year after they retire. They are so accustomed to working, and their identity is so closely tied to their job, that when they stop working their perceived purpose for living also stops.

The importance of work must be kept in balance with the other areas of one's life. God said in His Word that man and woman would toil and labor, and that labor and work are very good. Yet, work alone cannot be the only beneficial and fulfilling part of life.

When Jim was finally able to look at his situation and deal with his anger, he became director of a new business venture, but before he could move on with his life, it was necessary for him to RECOGNIZE (watch how many times in this book that this is the necessary, first step to getting well) that the old part of his life was over. Then he had to be willing to DECIDE (another step that pops up quite often) to move forward without resentment and anger.

Some of the major significant situations that trigger the grief process are:

Loss Of Our Youth (Through Aging Or A Decline In Our Abilities)

We live in a youth conscious culture. So much emphasis on television and in magazines is placed on staying young, fit, and vibrant. I am not against keeping our temples fit, but the obsession we have with health, fitness, and narcissistic self-preservation has taken on extreme proportions in Western society.

Our culture is so youth-oriented that growing old is often looked on as a plague. To stay young, we are encouraged to work-out, run, starve ourselves, use youth creams, buy younger clothes, drink the "in" colas, and get any face-lift, nose job, or breast implant which will somehow preserve our youth!

It is time that we as a society, begin to recognize that wisdom and experience are the most productive benefits that come with aging (in most cases), and that these qualities are to be appreciated and given their due respect.

The righteous man will flourish like the palm tree, He will grow like a cedar in Lebanon.

Planted in the house of the LORD, They will flourish in the courts of our God.

They will still yield fruit in old age; They shall be full of sap and very green,

To declare that the LORD is upright; He is my rock, and there is no unrighteousness in Him (Psalm 92:12-15).

In recent years there seems to be some shift in thinking about the value of older people in the work place. President Ronald Reagan, at the age of seventy-five managed the office of President of the United States. One of the largest organizations in the United States is the Association of Retired People. Another group, the "Gray Panthers," is also doing their part to inform the country that senior citizens no longer will allow themselves to be labeled as old and useless but as valuable and productive, especially in the areas of counseling others who lack experience and wisdom on how to direct their lives.

Companies like Wal-Mart, McDonalds and others are hiring senior citizens because they have found that, as a rule, they are much more reliable than many of the younger people they hire.

One of the stark realities of life we all must face is that our physical abilities do diminish. How you run and move in older age is drastically different than how you could run and move when you were ten years younger. When men reach the mid-life crisis, and women experience the "empty nest" syndrome, their limitations become even more evident, or at least they become more sensitive to those limitations.

It is important that we realize there is a normal grief process that we often experience with regard to the loss of our youth. Again, we must say good-bye to youth and hello to the new and wonderful things we can now do because of our increased wisdom and knowledge (hopefully).

Those people who are able to accept the limitations and realities of life in their older years tend to move through those years with more grace, with wonder, with a sense of joy and purpose. They learn to do things better, rather than harder and faster, than they did when they were younger.

Job or Occupational Loss

Many employees feel overworked, underpaid, and under appreciated yet their work is still a most important and needful endeavor in life. If the time comes when they become unemployed, the loss can be devastating, especially for men who have been socialized to believe that their self-worth is directly related to their occupation or level of income.

In America, men are raised with the myth that their worth is measured by how well they provide for and protect their families. God says differently. We are worthwhile because we are created in His image. SHOCK -- LOSS -- GRIEF -- are all emotions that may occur along with severe depression, when employment ceases. Many believe that their self-worth is gone (especially men who are taught since birth that they are to be the "bread winners" -- and when they are not working subsequently are considered a "bread loser"), and their purpose for living ceases with their last paycheck.

I once knew a young man whose personality was directly determined by the amount of money he had in his wallet. When he was down to a $5 or $10 dollar bill, he became tentative, uncertain, almost timid in his conversations, but put a $100 bill in his wallet and you could see the change. Suddenly, he was confident, fun to be with, and an excellent conversationalist. This man had taken his "self-worth" to the lowest possible measurement -- how much cash he had in his pocket.

As I mentioned earlier, one of the most vulnerable times for males is the first year after retirement since the "loss of job" often equates with the loss of self-worth and identity. It is important for men and women to reevaluate their true goals in life and realize that they have a worth that is GREATER than ANY job.

Remember, what you value most will dictate how you live your life.

If loss of employment occurs (and it will, whether it be through career changes or retirement), it is imperative that you learn how to say good-bye to the past, let go of what was, and move forward in faith and expectancy. With God's help and the guidance of friends, this transition in life can occur without too much pain.

Loss Of Goals

When we set goals and either achieve them or fail to achieve them, in either case there still tends to be a time of disappointment and emotional let-down.

For example, when a person completes a complicated educational program, it can trigger a sense of identity crisis. The same is true with a highly desired promotion. Once the goal is achieved, there can be a sense of loss of purpose for the individual's life.

Permit me to use myself as an example. I had been working towards completing the course requirements and dissertation for my doctorate in counseling psychology for over four and a half years. During this time, I had been dreaming, thinking, and fantasizing about being "Dr." Stan DeKoven.

When I finally accomplished my goal and received my doctorate, there was a strong feeling of "Is that all there is?" It took some time for me to realize that once I had achieved this major life goal, there were indeed more worlds to conquer, and that my life did not end with the achievement of my degree.

This success or failure principle applies to any goal that motivates a person. As we look forward, we tend to function well, but once the goal is removed, through achievement or failure, there is a strong sense of loss that still must be worked through.

Loss Of Self

God created us as very complex human beings. We are made up of body, soul (mind, will, and emotions), and spirit, the part of us which is in contact with God. Because we are so complex, when we experience a loss, we often experience a wound in our own identity that can be devastating to our self-esteem and self-respect.

Loss leads to grief and can additionally open us up to depression and despair. It is vital that we learn to deal with the multitude of losses that we may experience in this life. The Apostle Paul said that although he went through peril and distress, he could put those things aside and move forward in Christ.

> *"For I am convinced that neither death, nor life, nor angels, nor principalities, nor things present, nor things to come, nor powers, nor height, nor depth, nor any other created thing, shall be able to separate us from the love of God, which is in Christ Jesus our Lord."*
> (Rom 8:38-39 NASB)

Although, in this chapter, I have covered the four major areas in which a person can experience loss -- and the related pain and grief that comes with each type -- the list is certainly not exhausted. Obviously, there are many other areas in which a person can experience loss. The loss of an arm or leg due to an accident, the loss of sexual potency for men due to diabetes or other physical disorders, the loss of motherhood potential for women who cannot have children, the loss of ones childhood caused by abuse or abandonment in early life are just a few of the others areas of loss that have not been covered.

But they ALL have one thing in common -- you will experience GRIEF in almost any type of loss -- and the biblical prescriptions for "grief relief" contained in this book will help you ease your pain.

The goal is to RECOGNIZE the loss process, learn biblical keys for grief relief, and then experience the words of Psalm 51:12

> *"Restore unto me the joy of thy salvation; and uphold me with thy free spirit."*

Now, let us begin to understand the nature of grief.

Chapter Three

Understanding Grief

No one of us is immune to grief. Grief comes to everyone, and it comes in many different ways.

In this book, you have already seen that no matter how you experience the pain of loss -- through the death of a loved one, the loss of a job, a divorce, or the death of a pet -- the grief cycle triggers a myriad of emotions. So, as you read through the various steps, you may want to apply them to any significant loss in your life that you may have experienced.

Grief is unique, and each of us responds to it in different ways. Much of our response to grief is based on our incorporated belief system, that is -- how our parents, church and other social/cultural influences have taught us to respond. However, there are some common traits which we can draw upon to help us understand most of the common attributes of grief.

Common Myths about Grief

- All losses are the same.
- All bereaved people grieve in the same way.
- It takes two weeks to three months to get over your grief.
- When grief is resolved it never comes up again.
- It is better to put painful thoughts out of your mind.
- Anger should not be a part of your grief.

- Children need to be protected from grief and death.
- You will have no relationship with your loved one after death.
- The intensity and length of your grief are a testimony to your love for the deceased.
- Only sick people have physical problems in their grief.
- Funerals and rituals are unimportant in helping us heal.
- It is best to stay in control and keep a "stiff upper lip."
- It is best to put the memories of your loved one in the past and go on with your life.
- It is best to get involved and stay busy.
- Crying doesn't solve anything.

It is not easy to change traditions and long held beliefs or expectations. But, when we believe it is important for us and that it is in our best interest, we can re-learn and make changes. One difficulty is that we are impacted by the beliefs and feelings of those around us. While we may wish to change, others around us may not. It may take preparation and discussion to make changes, yet the results often benefit the whole family[2].

---

[2] Healing Through Grief. Editor: Kay Coggswell, LCSW, contributions by: Barbara Smith, MFCC; Scott Johnson, MA; Kathy Olsen, MA. Hospice of Grossmont Hospital and Sharp HealthCare is grateful for the collaboration of the Elizabeth Hospice and staff including Dorris Kingsbury, MFCC, and River malcom, MFCC Copyright 1995 Sharp HealthCare.

Grief Is Painful

The initial response to grief is simple -- it hurts! You may feel a tightness in your stomach or in your throat. You may experience persistent headaches or nausea. You may notice a dryness in your mouth. Your body may not move as you want it to. You may feel shortness of breath as if you need to breathe deeply or to sigh.

King David experienced intense grief at the loss of his son. As with most fathers his son was the love of his life, and the grief that he experienced is a feeling common to all of us. God's Word details for us both David's loss of a child and his reaction to it.

*Then the Lord sent Nathan to David. And he came to him, and said, "There were two men in one city, the one rich and the other poor.
"The rich man had a great many flocks and herds.*

"But the poor man had nothing except one little ewe lamb which he bought and nourished; And it grew up together with him and his children. It would eat of his bread and drink of his cup and lie in his bosom, And was like a daughter to him.

"Now a traveler came to the rich man, And he was unwilling to take from his own flock or his own herd, To prepare for the wayfarer who had come to him; Rather he took the poor man's ewe lamb and prepared it for the man who had come to him."

Then David's anger burned greatly against the man, and he said to Nathan, "As the Lord lives, surely the man who has done this deserves to die.

"And he must make restitution for the lamb fourfold, because he did this thing and had no compassion."

Nathan then said to David, "You are the man! Thus says the Lord God of Israel, 'It is I who anointed you king over Israel and it is I who delivered you from the hand of Saul.

'I also gave you your master's house and your master's wives into your care, and I gave you the house of Israel and Judah; and if that had been too little, I would have added to you many more things like these!

'Why have you despised the word of the Lord by doing evil in His sight? You have struck down Uriah the Hittite with the sword, have taken his wife to be your wife, and have killed him with the sword of the sons of Ammon.

'Now therefore, the sword shall never depart from your house, because you have despised Me and have taken the wife of Uriah the Hittite to be your wife.'

"Thus says the Lord, 'Behold, I will raise up evil against you from your own household; I will even take your wives before your eyes, and give them to your companion, and he shall lie with your wives in broad daylight.

'Indeed you did it secretly, but I will do this thing before all Israel, and under the sun.'"

Then David said to Nathan, "I have sinned against the Lord." And Nathan said to David, "The Lord also has taken away your sin; you shall not die.

"However, because by this deed you have given occasion to the enemies of the Lord to blaspheme, the child also that is born to you shall surely die."

So Nathan went to his house. Then the Lord struck the child that Uriah's widow bore to David, so that he was very sick.

David therefore inquired of God for the child; and David fasted and went and lay all night on the ground.

And the elders of his household stood beside him in order to raise him up from the ground, but he was unwilling and would not eat food with them.

Then it happened on the seventh day that the child died. And the servants of David were afraid to tell him that the child was dead, for they said, "Behold, while the child was still alive, we spoke to him and he did not listen to our voice. How then can we tell him that the child is dead, since he might do himself harm!"

But when David saw that his servants were whispering together, David perceived that the child was dead; so David said to his servants, "Is the child dead?" And they said, "He is dead."

So David arose from the ground, washed, anointed himself, and changed his clothes; and he came into the house of the Lord and worshipped. Then he came to his own house, and when he requested, they set food before him and he ate.

Then his servants said to him, "What is this thing that you have done? While the child was alive, you fasted and wept; but when the child died, you arose and ate food."

And he said, "While the child was still alive, I fasted and wept; for I said, 'Who knows, the Lord may be gracious to me, that the child may live.'

"But now he has died; why should I fast? Can I bring him back again? I shall go to him, but he will not return to me."

Then David comforted his wife Bathsheba, and went in to her and lay with her; and she gave birth to a son, and he named him Solomon. Now the Lord loved him and sent word through Nathan the prophet, and he named him Jedidiah for the Lord's sake.

(2 Sam 12:1-25 NASB)

Physical responses to loss are a normal part of the initial grief reaction.

Grief Is Directional

Grief moves naturally through several stages to a point where you accept your loss and begin to feel and act like your former self. We will examine this stage

56

in greater detail later. If you are feeling intense pangs of grief right now, the important thing to know is that your pain may be a strong indication that you are moving through a healthy, natural process.

Grief Is Personal

No one feels grief exactly as you feel it! Your feelings and your circumstances are unique. You must not fall into the trap of thinking you are alone and isolate yourself from others. Although they may not be openly grieving now, most of your friends have experienced some sort of grief, and they can help you. Let them help! Withdrawing from those who love you will only intensify the pain you feel and prolong the healing process.

Grief Moves Slowly

When a loved one dies, or when you experience any other significant loss, do not act as if nothing has happened. Your loss is difficult and significant, because it is personal; it happened to you.

It is natural that almost everything else may seem suddenly unimportant, such as your job, other family members, or even your familiar daily tasks. You may be anxious to overcome this feeling of meaninglessness. However, it is important to recognize that this lack of interest in other things is a natural feeling.

You must try to keep in mind that grief moves slowly and that a sense of personal meaning in your life returns slowly. You must not condemn yourself for not meeting some imaginary timetable of how long your grief should last.

A close friend of mine had spent nearly five years in full-time ministry when a public agency said he couldn't do his work any more. His loss was so powerful that he sat on the couch for nearly three months, depressed and in despair -- so many of his hopes and dreams seemed shattered. He felt abandoned, alone, and lost.

But with time, he was restored. His former ministry was but a mere shadow of his present work.

Grief Includes Mixed Feelings

Grief

Websters New World Dictionary (Warren Books. 1987) defines grief as "an intense emotional suffering caused by a loss."

The pain and hurt of grief is a very common feeling. Grief brings with it that feeling of emptiness and an aching pain in the gut. There is no instant cure for this experience. Time will heal it naturally.

The grief experience may also include other feelings such as guilt and hostility which are sometimes not accepted as "normal" in our Christian culture (as Christians, many say we should "rejoice" that our loved one has gone to be with the Lord -- without ever allowing time to mourn the physical separation).

Guilt, Hostility, and Anger

Almost every grieving person feels some guilt and anger, and it is often directed at God!

Have you ever asked, "Why did this happen to me?" So does almost everyone else. Let me share with you a typical example of how this reaction works.

A young woman's husband has died. She is now required to make several major adjustments rather rapidly. She suddenly becomes both mother and father to her children. She must find work, and she may be forced to sell the home in which she has lived for most of her married life. She will need to make many other severe adjustments, because there is usually insufficient money to handle these major changes.

These sudden and frequently drastic demands may cause the young lady to become angry. This anger is both normal and understandable. The best thing she can do is to express this anger openly to a trusted friend or to a competent counselor.

This anger should not be hidden. Hiding or repressing your anger only makes it worse, and it will surface at some other time in your life -- usually against someone who does not deserve to be on the receiving end of your angry outburst.

During the grieving process, it is natural for a person to feel hostility -- hostility directed toward the deceased, toward God, toward the boss who fired you from your job, or toward the world in general. This is a transitory response to the tremendous and significant loss you have suffered.

To the grieving person, death or any other loss experienced always seems completely unfair. Hostility or anger is to be expected. Hostility only becomes a problem when it becomes a constant and excessive feeling of anger that lasts over a long period of time. In this case the anger will gradually turn to bitterness that can have a long lasting, negative impact.

Remember, it is natural for your most frequent questions to be "Why?" "Why did God do this to me?" "Why is life so unfair?" These questions really mean, "I am angry because this terrible event happened to me." This is a normal response. Only when it becomes unresolved, and drags on for prolonged periods, will it give bitterness an opportunity to develop. The Bible wisely warns of the dangers of unresolved anger:

> *"In your anger do not sin: Do not let the sun go down while you are still angry, and do not give the devil a foothold" (Ephesians 4:26-27, NIV).*

Grief is an internal agony. The external projection of your anger onto others can exacerbate the problem. Occasionally, a hostile, grieving person can become unknowingly abusive to others. The anger of a widow or other person who is suffering from loss, often causes them to function with clouded thinking which in turn, can cause such extreme behavior as screaming and yelling. It is acceptable to express anger, but only if it is controlled, and is of a short duration.

Forgiveness, and letting go of hostility, are necessary in order to resolve your grief. You need to forgive your former spouse who divorced you. Forgive your former boss who fired you. Forgive your deceased spouse for leaving you so suddenly. And then move on with your life. Of course, forgiveness is not an event, but a process, and is required for healthy growth.

Grief Is Natural And Healthy

Grief is a natural and healthy response to a significant personal loss. As you try to think about grief as natural and healthy, consider these following situations. They are all part of the normal grief process. There are several normal reactions that a person may experience. They include the following:

"I Can't Talk"

You may find it extremely difficult to talk about your deceased loved one or other significant loss. For a period of time you may say to others, "I'm sorry, I just do not want to talk about it." This is perfectly all right. Eventually, however, you will WANT to talk about your loss, but you will know when it is that time. Do not permit your friends to force you into discussing your loss before you feel ready.

Time will eventually heal this natural reaction to death or loss, and in time you will talk about it!

One grieving woman I knew was very close to her older sister. When that older sister died of cancer, the younger woman avoided all conversations about the deceased sister.

She would constantly change the subject when it related to her older sister. She simply did not want to deal with the loss, and so she strenuously avoided any talk of the matter for several weeks.

Obsessive Reactions

You may find yourself eating, even when your food tastes bland and uninteresting. Under severe stress we tend to regress toward behaviors that give us a quick sense of comfort.

Eating is one of the earliest and most common behaviors that gave us a sense of warmth and well-being, so it is common to latch on to this behavior during the grief process. This stage is also a transitory part of the grief process.

Out of Touch

You may look at a letter from a friend without reading it, almost as if neither you, nor the letter are really there. A friend may be talking to you for ten minutes and you may not hear a word. You might be driving to an appointment and drive right past the place where you were supposed to go. All of these reactions are normal, due to a temporary lack of concentration. In time, this too will disappear.

Talking Out Loud

You may find yourself talking to your lost loved one, out loud, as though he or she were still present. You may find yourself arguing with your old boss, trying to convince him that you should not have been fired. You may catch yourself criticizing your ex-spouse out loud in an empty room for "something else" you just thought about that makes you angry. It should be comforting to know that you are not really crazy. You need to relax. This is simply a normal part of the process.

Memories

You may feel stabbing grief when you see a reminder of your loved one, such as a photograph, a stamp collection, or a best friend, even after you thought you had accepted your loss and returned to normal.

In divorce, old places trigger old memories -- especially old friends who you unexpectedly meet at the market or church. Many people who experience divorce find it necessary to make a whole new set of friends to escape the constant reminders of the departed spouse.

Reactions

You may laugh out loud in a room when you think about funny memories involving you and the person who has died. At the same time, you may feel guilt for laughing irreverently.

Forget the guilt. This is a normal reaction. Laughter also occurs at funerals -- where a person laughs almost without control. This is often misinterpreted as a lack of respect. IT IS NOT! In some individuals it is simply one way that the nervous system tries to cope with the stress of loss. It is much the same as the way that teenagers will giggle or laugh out loud when they are embarrassed in front of their friends by their parents.

Humor often helps us experience GRIEF RELIEF during the difficult days of adjustment after the loss of a job, a death, or any other significant loss.

Withdrawal

You may try to withdraw from those around you. Withdrawal, like denial, takes many forms. You may withdraw from the pain of grief by turning to alcohol or other drugs.

You may try to escape grief by over-activity, such as throwing yourself into your work or joining clubs or groups (over-committing your time so you do not have to feel the pain of grief).

You may even temporarily contemplate suicide, the ultimate attempt to withdraw. In these times, always call on Jesus Christ for strength, **and** seek counseling.

"(For the choir director. A Psalm of David.) In Thee, O LORD, I have taken refuge; Let me

never be ashamed; In Thy righteousness deliver me.

Incline Thine ear to me, rescue me quickly; Be Thou to me a rock of strength, A stronghold to save me.

For Thou art my rock and my fortress; For Thy name's sake Thou wilt lead me and guide me.

Thou wilt pull me out of the net which they have secretly laid for me; For Thou art my strength.

Into Thy hand I commit my spirit; Thou hast ransomed me, O LORD, God of truth. (Psalms 31:1-5 NASB)

If you tend to withdraw, and if it is keeping you from the normal functioning of life, you need to seek professional help. You need to reach out -- no matter how awkward it feels or how much it hurts. There are people who care and can help you. God cares about you and He has others prepared to assist you through your mourning process.

Self-pity

You may experience self-pity. Grief hurts; give attention to your pain. You are expected to take care of your emotional wounds. However, self-pity becomes a problem when, months after the death, or other significant loss, your consistent conversation starter is something like this: "No one knows how hard life is for me."

The person mired in self-pity then proceeds to recite a list of all the bad things that have happened to them. This process is futile; instead of helping, it only serves to perpetuate the pain. Perhaps the best scripture for counseling in almost every situation applies very well here:

> *Finally, brethren, whatever is true, whatever is honorable, whatever is right, whatever is pure, whatever is lovely, whatever is of good repute, if there is any excellence and if anything worthy of praise, let your mind dwell on these things* (Phil 4:8 NASB).

What a powerful bit of advice that is -- and if you apply the principles in that scripture, GRIEF RELIEF will flow into your life!

Normally, self-pity is used as a device to get the attention that you feel you lack because of your loss. Self-pity blinds you to the good things in your life, both with things as they were with your deceased loved one and in your life as it is now. You need to seek positive ways to get the attention you need, such as saying to a friend, "I need a hug," or to occupy your time by inviting a friend for dinner or out to a show. You need to do positive things that make you feel good and provide to you constructive attention.

These eight varied reactions are not all inclusive -- you may experience other reactions. Are they normal? Yes! Are they healthy? Yes, if they are allowed to flow within reasonable time frames. All of these reactions are normal and healthy, and are part of the process of moving through the grief experience.

Guilt -- A Useless Emotion

During your period of grieving for a significant loss, you probably will experience some guilt. Your guilt is a problem when it controls or dominates you, or when it blinds you to the possibility of resolving your grief and returning to normal patterns of living.

I know of a mother who reluctantly gave her son permission to buy a motorcycle, knowing that if she did not grant the permission, the son would have found a way to get the motorcycle anyway. About six months after the boy had the bike, he was in a fatal accident. When the woman finally entered counseling, she had spent over four years mourning the loss of her son -- and blaming herself through guilt for the accident (after all, she gave him permission to buy the motorcycle).

During this period of guilt, her husband divorced her, and her friends ceased to visit her. She became a hermit and ruined her own life -- feeling guilt over the death of a son -- yet her guilt was useless -- her son was gone, and nothing she could do would change that.

It is important to remember that Jesus died for ALL of our sins -- and He does not want us to become debilitated by guilt and condemnation. He loves you and freely pardons any transgression you might commit. If Jesus can forgive you, then you can forgive yourself. You must reach out to Him, for He is there for you during the "valley" of your "shadow."

Many of my clients who are struggling through the grief process make statements like these:

> "If I had taken my loved one to the hospital sooner, my spouse might have lived."

> "Maybe we should have found another doctor."

> "I shouldn't have pushed so hard. The strain and pressure I put on him caused the heart attack."

> "If I would have worked harder, I wouldn't have lost my job."

> "My child would be alive today, if I had fixed that car."

Do these or variations of them sound familiar? Thoughts like these are certainly understandable during the times of crisis, and the guilt which accompanies them is a very normal response. Some guilt is usually caused when a grieving person feels closed off or set apart from others. Often, they will feel like shouting, "I hurt, don't you understand that?" Or, "How can you act as if nothing has happened? I hurt!"

And then they feel guilty for needing to call attention to their own pain.

Yes you will hurt. You are rightly self-absorbed because you must be concerned about taking care of your emotional wounds. Expect to feel some guilt and to have second thoughts about your relationship with the deceased, or to think differently regarding the loss experienced. But it is vital that you achieve victory over guilt, especially since this type of guilt is one emotion that serves absolutely no constructive purpose.

Fear can prepare you for an impending danger. Anger can make you fight in unpleasant or undesirable circumstances, but guilt is useless -- it serves no purpose.

Because of Jesus' atonement, we can be set free from irrational guilt. To free yourself from useless guilt, take the following steps:

Step One

Acknowledge your need for forgiveness, either of your "sin," or your partner's, or others, and forgive.

Step Two

Forgive yourself, first express the negative feelings about yourself that have been causing the guilt, then forgive yourself for these transgressions.

Step Three

Accept the Lord's forgiveness according to the Word of God.

"If we confess our sins, he is faithful and just to forgive us our sins, and to cleanse us from all unrighteousness" (I John 1:9).

Step Four

If you rebuke and resist Satan, he must flee! We have God's promise. When Satan tries to dump the guilt your way, remind him of God's Word in this regard.

"Submit yourselves therefore to God. Resist the devil, and he will flee from you" (James 4:7).

Step Five

You must cast down (confess, talk about, throw down) vain (useless) imaginations or thought patterns. In II Corinthians chapter 10 and verses 4-5 we find,

"(For the weapons of our warfare are not carnal, but mighty through God to the pulling down of strong holds;) Casting down imaginations, and every high thing that exalteth itself against the knowledge of God, and bringing into captivity every thought to the obedience of Christ;

When your thoughts begin to dwell morbidly on your "worthlessness," you must cast down those thoughts and embrace what God says about you. Thoughts such as: "you are loved by God" (John 3:16); "You are fearfully and wonderfully made (Psalm 139:14); You are a new creation in Christ (II Cor 5:17); are the kinds of thoughts you should focus upon.

Grief Often Brings Denial

Some forms of denial over the death of a loved one, the break-up of a marriage, or even the loss of a job, are very natural. This is particularly true in the early stages of grief. Denial becomes a problem only when it is prolonged or extreme.

I have counseled with women who have been separated from their husbands for two or three years and still deny that their marriage is over. They stubbornly cling to a never-never land hope that their husbands (who are usually remarried or living with other women) will someday wake up and see the error of their way. Naturally, this type of "denial behavior" is out of balance and must be stopped.

Denial of death for months and years after the departure of a loved one usually means that the bereaved person is also denying other important aspects of life, such as personal appearance or healthy relationships with others.

If this is a problem, talk it over with someone you can trust and who will be honest with you. Your pastor or good Christian counselors are the kind of people who can help.

"Precious in the eyes of the Lord are the death of his saints" (Psalm 116:15)

Stan E. DeKoven, Ph.D.

Chapter Four

The Bible and Grief

Many well meaning, but ill informed, pastors and lay leaders have taught that if we are true Christians, grief, mourning, and the experience of loss should not be experienced. Since Christians are triumphant over death, and since heaven is assured, we should rejoice over the loss of a believing spouse, friend, or child. Unfortunately, these well meaning individuals have missed the whole council of God. Grief is a biblical concept. We see it throughout the Bible as we will discover here.

Old Testament Pictures

In the Old Testament nine different words are translated as "grief" from the original Hebrew. They are as follows:

- *Morah,* which is translated to mean bitterness or trouble (Genesis 26:35),
- *Kaac,* meaning vexation, anger, angry indignation, provocation, sore, sorrow, spite, wrath (Job 6:12; I Samuel 1:16; Psalm 6:7; 31:9).
- *Puwgah,* is translated to mean a stumbling block.
- *Makob,* is translated as anguish, affliction, pain and sorrow (2 Chron. 6:29; Psalm 69:26),

73

- **Kaeb,** is translated as suffering adversity both mental and physical (John 2:13; 16:3).
- **Yagown,** translates to affliction and sorrow (Psalm 31:10; Jeremiah 45:3).
- **Chalah,** which stands for a primitive root to be rubbed or worn, or figuratively to be weak, sick, afflicted, to grieve, to make sick, also to stroke or flattering (Isaiah 17:11; 53:10),
- **Choliy,** meaning malady, anxiety, calamity, disease (Isaiah 53:3; Jeremiah 6:7,10-19).
- **Yagah,** has the meaning to grieve, sorrow or vex (Lam. 3:32).

Job suffered great grief as did Jacob over his seeming loss of Joseph, as did David over the loss of his baby. In Isaiah chapter 53 we see that grief from loss was a characteristic that would be seen in the life of the Messiah. The experience of grief varied from sorrow to anxiety, illness, affliction, adversity, anguish, bitterness, anger, indignation, trouble and it was experienced as a stumbling block to enjoying life.

New Testament

The Greek words for grief and sorrow include **lupeo,** which means to distress, to be sad or to cause grief (2 Cor. 2:5). The expression of grief is found in the word **stenazo,** which is to sigh, to murmur, pray audibly with grief, groans and grudge (Hebrews 13:17). The word **lupe,** which is translated sadness, grief, heaviness and sorrow (I Peter 2:19). The Apostle Paul and Peter both described (and no doubt experienced) grief. However, none of the New Testament characters experienced grief and loss like Jesus did. At the grave of Lazarus, in the garden of Gethsemane, and certainly on the cross, Jesus experienced intense grief and loss, however, He was in every way the consummate overcomer.

Mourning

The process of grief is often called mourning. There are several Old and New Testament words translated as mourning. It was Jesus, Himself, who taught on the mountain, *"Blessed are those who mourn, for they shall be comforted (Mat 5:4 NASB).*

What happens to those who never mourn?

Let us examine these important words regarding mourning. The first word found in the Hebrew is *caphad,* which means to tear the hair and beat the breast, also to lament, akin to that word is *nuwd,* meaning to console, to bemoan, flee and to be sorrowful. Further, we have *gadar,* which means to mourn or to cause to mourn, *naham,* to growl, mourn or roar, *ebel*, to lament, or mourn, *abal and abel,* to bewail, lament and mourn.

In the Hebrew tradition, mourning was not done in isolation but was open, loud, and filled with robust emotional expression.

In the New Testament there are two words, *pentheo* and *kopto,* meaning to grieve, to beat the breast, cut down and to mourn.

In both the Old and New Testaments, in the lives of both saints and sinners, the downcast and the divine, a common unavoidable response to loss was (and is today) grief and mourning. Though there may be no escaping the impact of loss, there is hope as we understand the stages of grief and learn to process through it appropriately with God's help.

Unfortunately for many, the lack of healthy grieving leaves one depressed, having never experienced the comfort of The Holy Spirit, who is readily available for us.

Chapter Five

The Stages Of Grief

Moving through the grief stages is not an automatic process. You will move through the stages in different ways and at a different pace than others. Even family members who experience the same loss do not experience the same exact stages, in the same exact way.

The circumstances of the death or any other type of loss will also cause you to move through these stages differently, for example: the depth of your relationship with the person who has died, their age, their relationship with God, the kind of death or loss -- all of these factors will modify your own personal experience.

Let us now look at some of the normal stages. These are the author's stages based partially on the work of Dr. Elizabeth Kubler-Ross. They occur in the grief relief process after any significant loss.

Stage One: SHOCK

The first stage in grief is shock. With shock, a kind of numbness envelops you.

Shock is nature's built in cushion, insulating us from the severity of the blow. Shock is a physical sensation, a "spaced-out" feeling, a tight knot in your stomach, or even the loss of your normal appetite.

You may notice that you become distressed over little things which normally would not mean that much to you. Such as throwing a major tantrum when you discover a minor problem -- perhaps it is the missing button on a favorite piece of clothing, or the failure of a child to take out the garbage -- little things, made almost intolerable from the sudden shock of loss.

Or, you may not be able to remember small, common things such as your own phone number, or the name of a friend you see almost every day. These "memory blocks" are also a normal part of the shock stage.

Nervous laughter also occurs during this first stage of grief.

When I first heard that I had not been accepted into my college of choice, my initial reaction was the inappropriate laughter of disbelief (a form of shock). I experienced shock in a similar way when my Grandfather passed away. He was very special to me, and I did not want to believe he was really gone -- and strange as it may seem, an almost uncontrollable laughter was my response.

Shock and numbness will not prevent you from doing what you must do. You will act, at least in part, instinctively. Whatever your situation, you will normally retain the capacity to be rational. The numbness will soon wear away, and real grieving will begin.

Even without these particular symptoms of shock, you still may cry out from your heart something like this:

"Oh no, I can't believe he (or she) is gone!" This too, is a form of shock.

In some cases, a person may act as if their loved one had not died for hours (normal) or even days (not so normal -- if this type of denial continues, help should be sought), or they will act as though the loss had not occurred at all.

When you are hurting, you may appear not to care about others, but you are relying on automatic behavior, without thinking, because you are in a state of shock.

During this stage you may say, "I don't know what is happening to me," or, "Why can't I do something, why can't I think this through?" or even, "Why don't I care about others?"

All of these reactions are normal for shock, the first stage of grief. In time, the shock will wear off and you will again come in contact with your real emotions.

Stage Two: DENIAL

Usually, the stage after shock is denial. Of course you understand intellectually what has happened through your loss. But on a deeper level, all of your habits and memories are denying the death or the loss that has occurred.

You may find yourself setting the wrong number of plates at the table, or saving bits of news for someone who will never again be able to hear them.

In one case, when a man lost his job, he kept working at home on a major business report for his previous employer that he "just had to finish," even though he was no longer employed. It was only after his wife confronted him loudly, protesting he had to "stop the denial behavior", that he finally broke down and cried, sobbing, "Why me? Why me?"

Denial in some form or another may surface for many months or even years. There is no set time schedule for moving through this stage.

Some deny the loss of death by staying away from the grave or other reminders of their departed loved one. Others leave the deceased's room unchanged for a period of time. But perhaps the most common form of denial is to simply change the subject whenever circumstances about the pain or loss come up.

How many times, when you have questioned a friend or relative about a shocking loss -- such as divorce -- have you heard the answer, "I don't want to talk about it."? This is normal denial, and will usually diminish after the pain subsides. If you do what feels proper for you as you move towards acceptance, everything will eventually return to normal. There are simply no absolute, right or wrong time frames for the process.

It is important to understand that keeping a few treasures and pictures in view indefinitely is not denial, but simply an affirmation and a reminder of the love you have shared. A part of you will always grieve, but soon you will be able to accept the death of the one you have loved through the love of Jesus Christ, who strengthens you.

Stage Three: FANTASY VS. REALITY

The third stage of your transition is a struggle between fantasy and reality (this can actually be seen as a component of denial).

One may find oneself experiencing some of these fairly typical reactions that I have had voiced by my clients:

> "When I get up and go to the kitchen for breakfast, I almost expect my spouse to be there, waiting to greet me with a morning kiss."

> "I caught myself looking around the backyard expecting to see my child out there playing. I even brought my child's bike in from the rain so it wouldn't rust."

> "I heard someone pull into the driveway, and for a moment I thought my sweetheart was home from grocery shopping."

> "I saw her walking in the supermarket, and from the back, I was sure it was my wife. I found myself walking faster to catch up to her, only to remember that my wife was dead."

Perhaps you find yourself doing, or wanting to do, the things the two of you have always done, such as getting the mail, going for walks, or paying bills together. These are short fantasies and are a very normal way of wishing that things were different -- wishing that your loved one was still with you.

Whether you only think of these fantasies or act them out, consider them as transitory -- they will pass. They are healthy ways of experiencing grief relief and only reflect the cry in your heart that you wish they had not gone.

To want everything to be the same in your life -- just as it was before the loss or death -- is very normal. Most people in the grief process move frequently in and out of these experiences, from fantasy to reality to fantasy, with little or no control over such movement.

Although this is frustrating and confusing at times, one must not become alarmed by the behavior. It is a very normal part of the process.

Stage four: GRIEF RELEASE

Sooner or later you will come to realize that your loss is real, and the pain of this reality will penetrate to your deepest self. You will sob and weep -- from deep within your inner self. Your feelings will come pouring out like a fountain of sorrow. You may experience what Nehemiah felt when he heard about the captivity of the Jews and the destruction of his beloved Jerusalem:

> *Now it came about when I heard these words, I sat down and wept and mourned for days; and I was fasting and praying before the God of heaven (Neh 1:4 NASB).*

Or you may feel much like the prophet Jeremiah felt when he said,

> *Oh, that my head were waters, And my eyes a fountain of tears, That I might weep day and night For the slain of the daughter of my people!* (Jer 9:1 NASB).

You may even feel as though you are losing control of your feelings and emotions, but this should not be of any real concern.

Since you first learned of your tremendous loss you have come through many stages. These stages may have taken hours, days, or weeks, but you have come a long way. All the normal emotions that have been denied through these first stages now express themselves -- it is a grief release. Let it flow. Let your emotions out! This is one of God's ways of cleansing you from the pain.

After this grief release, much of your physical and emotional pain will fade away. Certainly the most noticeable and obvious signs of grief, such as shortness of breath, nausea, or choking sensations, will disappear.

You need to beware of those who try to comfort you by saying, "Don't cry, you'll be all right," or "Don't worry, God will take care of you."

These comments are well-intentioned but are from misguided givers of advice (such as Job's comforters).

Crying should **not** be held back. Thinking that you are a "bad" Christian because you are not rejoicing that your loved one is with God is simply not good thinking. The devil must not be allowed to condemn you for a "loss of faith" because you are hurting; and while those around you are saying, "Trust God, trust God."

The grief you are experiencing is God's way of releasing your emotions and pain. You need the time to cry and release your feelings.

Yes, God has promised to take care of you, and one way He takes care of you is by allowing your grief to be eased through crying, by letting your feelings out so that you are free once again to express them.

If you severely cut your arm and the pain caused you to cry, no one would say that you needed to "trust God."

If it is alright to cry because of the physical pain from an injury, why is it less right to be able to cry over emotional pain? Emotional pain is no less real than the physical pain that comes from an injury.

You will always have the memories of the loss, but as it is with a scar from a wound long since healed, you will eventually no longer feel the sharp pain.

Those who try to give you false comfort should not be rejected -- they are doing the only thing they know how to do to make you feel better. Being around someone who has just suffered a great loss is difficult for friends and acquaintances. It is hard at times, to know what to say, and often what is said may not be the best thing to say at that time. Without some real understanding of the grief process, it is difficult to be as supportive as you wish to be. There is good health in releasing your feelings and easing your grief, and this process in no way indicates a lack of faith or trust in God. In fact, it is actually harmful to hold these feelings inside.

A grieving person who keeps his feelings inside and delays their release for an extended period may experience some strong negative reactions, even manifested in physical problems such as ulcers, severe headaches, and other stress-related illnesses.

Stage Five: LIVING WITH MEMORIES

After you have experienced the therapeutic flood of grief from the previous stage, the pain of grief begins to ease. You are now emerging from the process to the victory of GRIEF RELIEF.

But the slow work of grief is not yet finished. When you go to church for the first time without your mate, you may feel the sharp pain of grief because of their absence from the seat beside you.

If a parent who has lived with you has died, you may be reminded of your loss when you receive a Christmas card addressed to them. When you drive by the building where you used to work before you were fired, pangs of anxiety and inadequacy may envelop you.

In ALL of these instances, you feel the hurt or grief again.

Naturally, on the first anniversary of the death of your loved one, you will be reminded of them -- and grieve. There will be more on surviving anniversaries in the section on caring for the bereaved (pg. 107). Naturally, when you meet an old work associate who reminds you of the job you once had -- you will grieve.

These experiences are very real, and a completely normal part of the grief relief process. Learning to live with memories is a long-term task. You will meet people, go places, and see things that remind you of your significant loss. But in this stage, painful grief is not a constant experience, it is aroused chiefly by specific incidents that trigger old memories.

Stage Six: ACCEPTANCE -- AFFIRMATION

In this stage, you are now beginning to accept the loss and to affirm in your own life that you will go on living.

Good memories of the deceased are brought to your mind without stabbing pain and often with gratitude and pleasure for such recollections.

If you have just lost a major job, after a period of mourning, there comes a time when you say, "That's it -- I have got to get on with my life."

When you are finally ready to decide to make that statement of acceptance such as, "I can't change it. It has happened, and it is over.", or a statement of affirmation such as, "It is time for me to get out and start dating again." -- then you are well on your way to a healthy, normal life.

I encourage you to entertain good memories. Good memories will make it easier and easier to talk about your loved one and to appreciate your past relationship without wishing unrealistically that it could be restored.

You will start to show a renewed trust in yourself, as if to say, "I can make it." No matter how you express it, there is great hope when you begin to see good possibilities for yourself and your future.

You need to remember that the process of grief relief often takes years to fully complete. There is no need to hurry it. Grief moves at its own pace.

By trusting in the Holy Spirit, you can dedicate your grief process to the will of God and trust He will do a good work in you.

> *For I am confident of this very thing, that He who began a good work in you will perfect it until the day of Christ Jesus* (Phil 1:6 NASB).

During this stage of affirmation and acceptance, you will begin doing more things with others. You may take your children to the beach -- and enjoy it. You may sponsor a wedding shower -- and not feel lonely for your ex-spouse.

You may go bowling with some of your former work associates -- without the strong pangs of remorse over the fact that you are no longer employed with their company.

You may reminisce about the good times you had with your spouse, and even laugh about some of the funny times -- without the hurt.

You are finding new meaning in what you do.

You can celebrate the memories of your deceased loved one without being obsessed by these memories. You can also celebrate the positive parts of your old job, your former spouse (in a divorce) without being obsessed by the negative factors in these events.

> *O give thanks to the LORD, for He is good;*
> *For His loving kindness is everlasting (1*
> *Chr 16:34 NASB).*

"There is a light in this world, a healing spirit more powerful than any darkness we may encounter. We sometimes lose sight of this force when there is suffering, too much pain. Then suddenly, the spirit will emerge through the lives of ordinary people who hear a call and answer in extraordinary ways."
Mother Teresa

Stan E. DeKoven, Ph.D.

Chapter Six

Grief Relief

Death is as much a mystery as it is painful and real. Death, and significant losses of any other type, leave us with a feeling of bewilderment and frustration.

As you grieve, you feel the mystery. You ask "Why?" and no one seems to have an adequate answer.

You hurt, and no one seems able to erase the pain.

But through the power of Jesus Christ, we can put death, or any loss, in the context of our Christian faith and hope. This will not automatically clear up the mystery, ease the pain, or give you faith and hope but, in time, the TOTAL VICTORY will be yours.

> *And after you have suffered for a little while, the God of all grace, who called you to His eternal glory in Christ, will Himself perfect, confirm, strengthen and establish you.*
>
> *To Him be dominion forever and ever. Amen. (1 Pet 5:10-11 NASB)*

Do you see it? Your Christian walk affirms death, loss, and grief as a natural part of life. The Christian faith sees death in two parts:

1. As the cessation of physical life, or
2. As alienation from God.

To a Christian, the only death that matters in the eternal framework of things is when we are alienated from God.

The threat of death, with both of its meanings, is the oasis for God's action in providing the means to salvation. Salvation through Jesus Christ is offered to save us from sin and death. As paradoxical as it seems, if there were no death, there would be no hope.

> *"He who has found his life shall lose it, and he who has lost his life for My sake shall find it.* (Mat 10:39 NASB)

The fact that death and grief are a part of the Christian life sets us free to accept loss by death, or any other loss, as natural and inevitable. Questions like, "Why did God let him die?" or "Why were my hopes lost?" take on new meaning. When you understand death from a Christian perspective, then anger at God, though being a somewhat normal response, is not a necessary one.

Loss is a natural part of life. Blame is not necessary when we accept a Christian view of death and dying.

> *We know that we have passed out of death into life, because we love the brethren. He who does not love abides in death* (1 John 3:14 NASB).

Christian fellowship is an affirmation of life. The Christian fellowship, through your local church, should demonstrate life out of death. During your grief relief period, your church community will hopefully say to you, "We stand with you and believe that God is the source of life. We comfort you in your grief. We want to provide you with a caring and supportive fellowship. We acknowledge your value as a person. We say to you that honesty, truth, caring, worship, and commitment are important to us, even in the face of loss or death. These values are alive in you. Your values have not been destroyed."

Do you see the great significance in Christian fellowship? This is seen in a simple truth from the Bible:

> *"And they continued in the apostles' doctrine and fellowship, and in breaking of bread, and in prayers" (Acts 2:42).*

You must not feel that you are a burden to your church community. You actually rob them of a blessing by refusing to accept their sincere help.

> *The one who does not love does not know God, for God is love* (1 John 4:8 NASB).

Your hope is found in your relationship with God. He is the source of your hope. God loves you. In your grief, this may not seem clear to you. Even Jesus, when he faced death on the cross, cried,

> *And about the ninth hour Jesus cried out with a loud voice, saying, "ELI, ELI, LAMA SABACHTHANI?" that is, "MY GOD, MY GOD, WHY HAST THOU FORSAKEN ME?"* (Mat 27:46 NASB).

Yet, this same Jesus, a short time later said,

> *And Jesus, crying out with a loud voice, said,*
> *"Father, INTO THY HANDS I COMMIT MY*
> *SPIRIT." And having said this, He breathed*
> *His last (Luke 23:46 NASB).*

When you yield to God, this victorious step guarantees that there is hope in the face of death and grief. Hope, death, and grief are natural. Hope remains after death and grief are gone.

> *But we do not want you to be uninformed,*
> *brethren, about those who are asleep, that you*
> *may not grieve, as do the rest who have no*
> *hope (1 Th 4:13 NASB).*

Neither death nor grief can separate us from God's love.

> *Who shall separate us from the love of Christ?*
> *Shall tribulation, or distress, or persecution,*
> *or famine, or nakedness, or peril, or sword?*
> *Just as it is written, "FOR THY SAKE WE*
> *ARE BEING PUT TO DEATH ALL DAY*
> *LONG; WE WERE CONSIDERED AS*
> *SHEEP TO BE SLAUGHTERED."*
>
> *But in all these things we overwhelmingly*
> *conquer through Him who loved us.*
> *For I am convinced that neither death, nor*
> *life, nor angels, nor principalities, nor things*
> *present, nor things to come, nor powers,*

nor height, nor depth, nor any other created thing, shall be able to separate us from the love of God, which is in Christ Jesus our Lord (Rom 8:35-39 NASB.

Recently, an evangelist related his personal experience after the death of his mother.

His mother had lived a long and fruitful life for the Lord, including many decades in her active evangelistic ministry. Though there was the normal grief response, in the midst of the sense of loss, he also experienced a sense of victory.

At the funeral there was little crying. In fact, the worship and message were so inspiring that nine of the people there accepted the Lord Jesus Christ as their own personal savior.

"O DEATH, WHERE IS YOUR VICTORY? O DEATH, WHERE IS YOUR STING?" (1 Cor 15:55 NASB).

Let me summarize some of the steps you can take to work through grief:

1. Don't ignore your feelings.
    Tears are normal, natural, and essential. Allow yourself the privilege of talking or crying. Denying your grief and the need to mourn can cause greater problems in the future. Give yourself permission to feel.

2. Do not punish yourself.
    Often we blame ourselves for real or imaginary
    wrongs which can keep us from being
    productive. We know that our Lord loves us
    unconditionally. Thus, we must work toward
    full acceptance of our loss and not hold
    ourselves responsible for what we can not
    change.

3. You are not alone.
    Though your loss is yours, you are not the only
    one who has experienced loss. Your pain is
    unique, yet, you are a part of the human
    condition.

4. Take time.
    Healing takes time. For major losses, it often
    takes up to two years to process through grief,
    and we will most likely never forget. You must
    tend to your emotional trauma as you would a
    physical wound. Thus, postpone major decisions
    in your life until your healing is well on its way.

The ultimate goal of this process is to find peace of
mind. This does not happen through a simple prayer,
trite phrases, or "just getting on with life." The longer
and more intimate the relationship -- the longer the
time to heal. Trust God in the process.

"I first thought that daddy died because I didn't do my homework. I got mad at him...that's why he went away. But I know that it is not true. I miss daddy, sometimes I'm scared." (William, Age 9)

Stan E. DeKoven, Ph.D.

Chapter Seven

What Do You Tell The Children?

Children know sorrow. Because children are small, many adults falsely assume that their hurts are also small.

But who can say with certainty that children suffer any less than adults do during a significant loss? Children are people too, and their needs should not and cannot be overlooked.

The question is, how do you tell a child that someone he or she loves, has died? How do you tell a child that Daddy will no longer be going to work at his old job -- that the company does not want him anymore?

It is difficult to do, but in almost all cases of significant loss, a straightforward approach is the best approach. Handled carefully, the truth should be good enough.

Your own belief system will, of course, determine what you say about the meaning of death and about life after death.

Your own attitudes will determine how much trauma a divorce or serious job loss will have upon the emotional world of your children. If the child hears a sobbing mother cry, "What will we do now? We have no money, and we have no food -- and now we have no job!" The child is very likely to think, in his mind, that he is about to starve to death. Children take things literally.

Careful selection of words when you share these significant losses with them will go far to avoid undue stress for the children. Hysterical distortion of the actual facts of the situation can cause lasting harm to the children.

For example, if you explain to a child that his Daddy has "gone to sleep" instead of saying "He has died", the young child could develop a fear of going to sleep from your softened explanation.

If you tell a child that "God needed your Mommy in heaven," the youngster may develop a hatred toward God for being so cruel and selfish as to take his mother away. After all, does God really need Mommy more than the lonely child?

If you tell your child that his mother, "died in a hospital," you must be careful to clarify that it was the illness that caused her death and NOT the hospital. Otherwise, the child may develop an abnormal fear of hospitals. The child needs to be reassured that not everyone who goes to the hospital dies.

These little tips might seem like minor considerations to some readers of this book, but to children who live in a very literal world -- who take everything adults say to heart -- these false interpretations of events in their minds are major considerations.

In a divorce situation, for example, where a child is perhaps losing his father's permanent presence in the home, an explanation like, "things will be fun in our new home," will only serve to confuse and frustrate his love for his father.

Children do not have the same feelings of hate and anger in a divorce as the parents have toward each other. The explanation the child hears must be tempered with wisdom and affection.

"Your father and I have tried very hard to make our marriage work, but for reasons we do not quite understand, we just keep hurting each other. To stop the hurts, the only thing left for us to do was to separate."

Now maybe those are not the exact words you would select, but when you do select your own words, make sure they are tempered with love (not anger), and understanding (not hatred), so the child does not visualize his world as being completely shattered. Many a mother has felt quite justified in telling her child, "Your father is no good! He beat me, slugged me, came home drunk, did not provide food for us, and slept with other women, so I told the bum to get out."

That explanation may help the mother vent some of her anger, and may indeed be true, at least in part, but it will not help a small child cope with the separation and loss of a father.

Instead, the mother needs to consider an explanation that goes something like this: "Your father needs to learn how to handle his temper. It is impossible for adults to live together if one is going to constantly hurt the other. Your daddy is bigger and stronger than I am, and yet somehow right now he is not able to stop hitting me. We've decided to separate so that I don't get hurt anymore and not be able to take good care of you. This will give him a chance to work on his problem with his temper. Our separation has nothing to do with you." Although the divorce may be necessary because the father is abusing the child, in which case this whole scenario would need to be different. "Daddy still loves and cares about you and will see you as often as he can. I still love and care about you and will do the best I can to make our life together the best it can be. Oh, I know it won't be easy, but together we will make it."

This is not to suggest that you should lie to your child. You simply must not explain the situation to him or her in the same bitter, angry voice and terminology that you would share the situation with a friend.

Yes, YOU may want to make the "louse" out to be a bad guy -- but to a child, that "louse" is STILL his daddy. Help the child to understand the truth and avoid coloring the truth with your own pain.

Your assurances of love and support are the greatest things you can give to a grieving child. They should be reminded that the loss of one important love relationship does not mean the loss of all others, including your own love.

Children must be assured that they were in no way to BLAME for either the death or divorce. It is natural for young children to think that anything bad that happens in their little world is somehow their fault. "If Daddy is beating Mommy, it must be because of something that I did."

If Mommy has died suddenly, "it is because God knows I have not been a good boy." It must be reinforced over and over that the divorce or death is in no way the fault of the child or caused by his behavior.

A very young child may naturally wonder, "Who will take care of me now?" He or she must be assured that their physical needs will be taken care of and that their life will change some, but it is not coming to an end.

Children should be allowed to participate in the family sorrow. If shielded, they may feel rejected, as though they do not belong. They may also feel that they are being blamed for the loss. They need to know that they are loved and needed.

It may be distressing to see a father cry, but it is far more distressing to see "business as usual" at a time of loss. Children are especially sensitive to insincerity.

Yes, you should share the reality with your child. And at the same time, try to protect the child from unnecessary burdens. For example, it is necessary to tell a child about the death of their father, but you must not say yourself nor allow others to say to that child, "You are my little man, and now YOU are the head of the house. It is up to YOU to take care of Mommy." That is too large an assignment for a little child, and instead of bringing comfort, it only brings fear and pain to their little hearts.

No child (or adult for that matter) should be told to "be brave." Instead the child should be allowed and encouraged to "let out his feelings." Children need to know that it is all right to cry and they need to be assured that you understand the hurt that they are experiencing. They also need to be assured that in time the hurt will not be quite so bad. As parents, we must be cautious not to create in the child's mind the idea that they should be feeling something when they are not. This could create guilt in the child's thinking because they do not feel what they are "supposed" to feel.

The adults in a loss situation must be careful not to put up a false front, because this only makes grieving more difficult.

One of the precious people the Lord has allowed me to work with related that she had been sent away to another city for her "protection" by her parents when her favorite grandmother had died. She never had the opportunity to say good-bye to the grandmother she dearly loved.

As a result of this seemingly sensitive action, deep fears and bitterness were planted in this young girl's mind and spirit, and they were not effectively dealt with until over twenty years later! During those twenty years, she had experienced untold hurt and anguish because of a misguided adult's need to protect her as a child. The child should be allowed to express his or her feelings. Children need to experience the finality of the loss.

It is acceptable for the child to feel anger. A child should never be punished for their expressions of anger without an awareness that their actions might be cries for help. Often children are unable to directly express their feelings through dialogue, so they seek outlets for their emotions through other behaviors.

A seventeen-year-old boy suddenly became a discipline problem in school, and openly hostile toward authority. His grades began to drop. At first the parents did not understand what was causing the problems, so they dealt with the situation in many of the old, standard ways. They grounded the young man. They forced him to sit at the table and study for two hours a night. They also took away his new car "until his grades went up", but nothing seemed to make a difference.

Finally, the father, sensing that there was something else going on, asked, "Son, would you like to go and talk with someone who could possibly help you get rid of all the anger you seem to have inside?"

To the father's complete surprise, the son immediately said he would. In professional counseling, it became evident that the boy was suddenly "angry" at adults because they had taught him how to pray for his sick aunt who died anyway! No one close to the boy realized that his aunt's death would have that much impact on him. After all, he only saw her a few times each year, and he did not appear to be especially close to her. Yet, her death was very traumatic to him.

Even at seventeen, many young boys and girls still are not able to verbalize why they are angry after a divorce or death -- they just feel the raw anger and know they have got to do something with it. This type of reaction is particularly common among adolescents. They are additionally dealing with many new and strange emotions because of the hormonal changes taking place in their bodies.

This type of anger is especially manifested in a child's play. By being sensitive to what a child is "saying" in their games -- since these actions are especially beneficial in determining how the child is adjusting to significant loss -- adults can often learn what the child is feeling. If the child is doing a lot of hitting with his toys, or on his playmates, he or she is probably experiencing hostility and anger and needs your help to begin releasing this anger in healthier way, such as a good sports workout or an old-fashioned wrestling match with Dad.

Of course you cannot encourage hostile behavior, but you do not want to compound the problem by telling the child what a "bad boy" or "bad girl" he or she is. Instead, the child should be allowed to know that hitting is unacceptable behavior. Then let him or her know that the hitting is caused by the anger they are feeling about something significant that has happened. Some-times an expression like, "You really miss your Daddy, don't you?" is the type of question that will open the door to a better understanding of the anger being felt by your child.

The key thing to remember here is that it is vital for you to temper discipline with love and understanding.

Providing an environment in which feelings can be expressed spontaneously, such as in open family talks, can give encouragement to children to express their feelings. As such, the parents are acting as models of open communication. If more than one child is involved in the crisis, time must be spent alone with each of them. The needs of one may be much greater than the needs of the others.

For example, the seventeen-year-old boy re-acted one way to his aunt's death, while other teenagers in the same family environment did not experience the same reaction.

In dealing with children, it is important to be aware that tears are not the only measure of grief. Unfortunately, the crying child gets the most sympathy, while the less demonstrative child will also need help. Withdrawal in time of emotional distress is common with young children and is much more hazardous potentially than the "acting out" behavior of other children.

Children should be allowed to share your own personal progress in the grieving process. As you work through your own loss, your child will be helped to do the same. You should find some activities that you can do together, and share your activities with your child. Taking the child to church with you, is a good example. If you need to run some errands, take them along. Companionship during this time is vital and nourishing.

Chapter Eight

How A Child's Death
Can Affect Your Marriage

This is a special chapter about a special circumstance. You should know that if a child in the family dies, all the previous information concerning the grief relief process applies, but one additional element is added. Your marriage is very likely to be severely strained.

In my years of counseling experience, the anticipated ideal of each spouse supporting and helping the other in encouragement and love after the loss of a child is rarely realized. Both parents are overwhelmed with grief; neither husband nor wife finds themselves in a position to give support to the other.

Each of the parents is experiencing so much grief individually that they have very little emotional strength left with which to support someone else. Parents in this kind of situation often cannot find the kind of support they need from their spouse. Help will of necessity, need to come from the outside. Each parent has a special and unique path of grief to follow. Each parent will feel the pain differently.

Accusation or Blame

Nothing is so devastating -- and common -- to the marriage of bereaved parents as blame. If you feel that your spouse is somehow responsible for your child's death, such as by not providing sufficient parental care, or because they failed to anticipate the accident, your marriage situation is probably precarious.

Few grieving parents can handle the guilt of accusation. In some cases, because one parent is not hurting in the same exterior manner as the other, they are told, "You never loved our child the way I did." Each parent is already experiencing an overwhelming load of responsibility, even when they could not be considered responsible for the tragedy. For the other parent to add to that feeling by accusing only compounds the guilt.

The best advice is "DO NOT ACCUSE!"

"Why do you look at the speck of sawdust in your brother's eye and pay no attention to the plank in your own eye?

How can you say to your brother, 'Brother, let me take the speck out of your eye,' when you yourself fail to see the plank in your own eye? You hypocrite, first take the plank out of your eye, and then you will see clearly to remove the speck from your brother's eye! (Like 6:41-42 NIV).

The Bible is crystal clear on this. You need to deal with your own set of hurts and emotions without blaming your spouse for their failures. That does not mean that you are to let your feelings smolder unexpressed. You need to get some constructive dialogue with an outside party such as a mental health professional, your pastor, or professional counselor who is trained and equipped to help you resolve the feeling of blaming.

Condemnation and criticism are **never** from the Lord. You must recognize that forgiveness is a commandment from God, not just a suggestion.

> "Do not judge, or you too will be judged. For in the same way you judge others, you will be judged, and with the measure you use, it will be measured to you. "(Mat 7:1-2 NIV)

> "Do not judge, and you will not be judged. Do not condemn, and you will not be condemned. Forgive, and you will be forgiven." (Luke 6:37 NIV).

The importance of forgiveness cannot be over emphasized. When Jesus taught his disciples to pray in Matthew chapter 6, the part of the prayer that He stressed most was that aspect detailed in verses 12-15 dealing with forgiveness:

> "Forgive us our debts, as we also have forgiven our debtors.

> And lead us not into temptation, but deliver us from the evil one.'

> For if you forgive men when they sin against you, your heavenly Father will also forgive you.

> But if you do not forgive men their sins, your Father will not forgive your sins" (Mat 6:12-15 NIV).

Receiving forgiveness as taught in this passage of scripture is contingent on our forgiving others. If we forgive, we shall be forgiven. This should make it obvious that the vital thing is for parents to be able to forgive each other for any actual or imagined fault in the death of their child.

A vicious cycle of condemnation begins to set in when one parent starts to blame the other. Invariably, as a matter of self-defense, the condemned party begins to look for areas in which they may be able to strike back, and the unhealthy process of accusation continues to intensify.

Communication

Often one spouse, or both, cannot seem to talk about the loss of their departed child. In my counseling, I have found that scheduling a certain daily time for such discussion has been a workable answer to help many parents get over this difficult adjustment. The "non-talking" parent can at least listen during these scheduled periods and then eventually, they will talk during other times as the grief relief process ensues.

Communication is the lifeblood of the marriage. Harboring grievances or bitterness can only result in serious marital problems. You should talk about your hurts and emotions openly, but without rancor, before you accumulate an entire bag full of bitterness. Learning to communicate positively with your spouse can prevent the root of bitterness getting a start and eventually springing up to produce destruction (see Hebrews 12:15).

These kinds of communication demand the cooperation of both parents. If one parent is reluctant to participate in the process, then by all means seek professional counseling before you find yourself starting to seek a divorce lawyer!

Other Problems

A long term illness within a family often leaves behind enormous financial difficulties. Since these difficulties are the result of an unusual circumstance, you might want to seek the help of a good financial counselor to help you solve this staggering problem. Often the financial counselor can make contacts with your various creditors and work out a plan that will effectively help you solve those problems without having to file for bankruptcy.

Another common problem during this difficult time is the lack of or diminishing in the desire for sexual intercourse. This may be natural, for a time, but if the sustained abstinence from sexual relations continues, it becomes a desperate situation which must be resolved. A malaise concerning your marriage has set in, coloring everything in blacks and browns. Many types of resentments and recriminations may surface.

If you find there are problems like these in your marriage, and no resolution is in process, outside help is urgently needed. Frequently, it is nearly impossible for the couple to work through these issues without help, because the emotions are too intense and there is limited past history in the successful resolving of such conflicts.

If there is little hope for clear vision and objectivity on your own, you need to locate a Christian counselor, family therapist, pastor, or even a compassionate friend, experienced in grief counseling. Often, a funeral counselor is available to listen and give help (although many find the environment of the funeral home too close a reminder of the death of the child).

The important thing is to do something soon. You should seek the help of someone who knows and understands what you are going through, and knows how to help you soften the hurts. Hopefully, you will only have to deal with this type of crisis once in your lifetime -- but the professional counselor has the experience of dealing with this crisis many times each year during the course of his or her normal caseload. The information they have gathered through these counseling experiences can and will help you to work through your own particular emotions.

You must remember, you have already lost a child -- that is tragic enough without adding to it the death of your own marriage.

The Loss Of An Unborn Child

One final loss that occurs in relationships, where the grief relief process must be applied, is when the parents have lost an unborn child. This is an often overlooked but extremely painful loss. It is as significant to the parents as the loss of any loved one.

In the dozens of cases that I have counseled, the mother (she experiences herself as such even if this is her first child) **always** knows that she was carrying within her a living gift from God. In many cases, she (and sometimes the father also) knows intuitively the gender of the miscarried child and has already developed a significant bond with the child (emotional /psychological attachment). When a spontaneous loss of the child occurs, the shock, hurt, anguish and sorrow can be almost overwhelming.

When a loss of this kind occurs, the stages of Grief Relief discussed here still apply. However, there is usually limited formal opportunity in our society to process through the loss. Thus, I strongly recommend to the parents of this "all too brief gift of life", that they hold a private memorial service for their child.

During this "service," usually held at home (though a park or even a church is quite suitable) is included: the naming of the child, a eulogy from the parents (What if? We miss you. What we had hoped for your life. etc..), a prayer of dedication of the child to God, and perhaps something symbolic, like lighting a candle. Ultimately, the goal, as with any other loss is the saying of good-bye to the loved one, releasing them into God's capable care, and going on to embrace life in all its uncertain mystery.

In giving care to a family who has had a loss of this nature, special care should be taken not to minimize the powerful impact of the loss.

Stan E. DeKoven, Ph.D.

Chapter Nine

Fifteen Tips To Expedite
The Grief Relief Process

Here are fifteen key ideas to keep in your mind when you are dealing with grief resulting from death or ANY significant loss -- such as divorce or the loss of a job.

This list of helpful ways to experience grief relief is the result of many years of helping hurting families and individuals. These principles have helped others, and I know they will help you.

1. Nurture Your Relationship With God

If you have been inactive in your relationship with God, there could never be a better time to become involved again with spiritual matters. The Bible is of great comfort and it has much to say about the nature of sorrow.

> *The righteous cry and the LORD hears,*
> *And delivers them out of all their troubles.*
> *The LORD is near to the brokenhearted,*
> *And saves those who are crushed in spirit.*
> *Many are the afflictions of the righteous;*
> *But the LORD delivers him out of them all.*
> (Psa 34:17-19 NASB)

Ironically, many who have not had a close relationship with God -- in the face of a death or other severe crisis -- will draw closer. Conversely, many who have been close to God sometimes are drawn away.

If you already have a strong relationship with God, you may experience a temporary distancing from Him during this time of grief transition.

One Italian family I was counseling experienced the loss of a forty-four-year-old daughter to cancer. All of the adult sisters and many of the nieces and nephews who had been praying for her recovery went through a time of "anger" at God for not allowing their sister or aunt to live.

However, over a period of time, most of these same people began to realize that cigarettes, not God, were the cause of the relatives death, and their love for God returned.

As time passes, you will find most people who are initially angry at God will release their anger and become close to Him again.

2. Accept The Grief

As I shared earlier in this book, during a significant loss is not the time to "try and be brave." Take the time to cry.

It is all right to hurt, and it is a necessary and natural process. Do not condemn yourself, or accept the condemnation of others because you are not "trusting in God" or are "lacking in faith." God has designed you to release your natural pain through real tears. Crying is necessary for both men and women -- strong men can and do cry (King David and the Lord Jesus Himself are classic biblical examples of this).

3. Talk About Your Loss

Share your grief within the family; do not attempt to protect each other by awkward silences. Find a friend to talk to, or anyone else who will listen to your hurts without passing judgment.

If possible, find someone who has experienced a similar sorrow and can share some common experiences with you. Once a person has experienced a significant loss, they understand what you are now going through, and can share some of their experiences with you.

4. Keep Busy

This sounds like avoidance, but it is not. I am suggesting that you find purposeful work that occupies your mind. When I suggest you "stay busy," I am not suggesting you buzz around in frantic, mindless activity. But when a "part of you" has died through loss of a loved one or another grief situation, it is vital that the "part of you" that is left, be somehow productive. Some suggestions:

- Work as a volunteer in a drug rehabilitation program.
- Serve as a driver for Meals on Wheels.
- Become a reader for the blind.

In short, pick healthy, worthwhile, activities centered upon others to occupy your time and keep your mind from meditating excessively on your own hurts. By meeting the needs of others, you will find yourself simultaneously meeting your own needs.

5. Take Care Of Yourself

Bereavement can be a threat to your health. At the moment, you may feel that "you don't care" about your body or your health. In fact, you may even be overeating to ease the pain -- and in the end, this negative type of activity will only make you feel worse. It is vital for you to realize that your needs are important.

Your life is valuable; care for it. Jesus valued you enough to give His life for you.

"But God demonstrates his own love for us in this: While we were still sinners, Christ died for us" (Rom 5:8 NIV)

You see, He loves you and sees you as infinitely important to himself.

6. Eat Well

At this time of emotional and physical depletion, your body needs good nourishment more than at any other time. Avoid fast-food solutions to your hunger whenever possible. Many people do not feel like cooking and turn to fast-food restaurants for quick meals. Fast-foods are typically high in fat, salt, and calories.

If you must avoid cooking, carefully select eating places that feature salad bars and food that is broiled rather than deep-fried. Fruits are an excellent source of vitamins during this time of non-cooking.

Loss of appetite may also be a problem. If you can only pick at your food, a vitamin supplement might be helpful, but it will not make up fully for a poor diet. If you sense your body is growing weaker and weaker, you may need to see your family doctor to ensure that your health is maintained.

7. Exercise Regularly

Return to your old exercise program, or start one as soon as possible. Depression can be reduced somewhat by the biochemical changes brought about by exercise. Studies in mental institutions and hospitals show that depression is often dramatically reduced by simple exercise such as jogging or walking.

If you exercise each day, you will also sleep better. An hour-long walk every day is ideal for most people, and if it is done with someone you like, it is also a great time to talk about the roller-coaster emotions you are now experiencing.

8. Get Rid Of Imagined Guilt

When a child or a spouse dies, sometimes those of us remaining experience different types of guilt.

"I just saw her yesterday, and we ended up fighting. Oh, if we hadn't had that fight, she might not have gone out drinking and could have avoided the accident."

"If I would have said no when my son asked for the motorcycle, perhaps he would be alive today."

"If only I would have been a more loving wife, and given him everything that he wanted, maybe my husband would not have left me for that younger woman."

All of these types of statements are non-productive and only serve to evoke useless feelings of inadequacy. They should be avoided at all costs.

If you lost a long-term job, remember the things you did right while you worked for your old employer. Do not dwell on the things that you did wrong. You will probably discover that you did the best you could at the time.

If you have made mistakes in your relationships, that is all right, also. We all must learn to accept that we are imperfect. Only hindsight is 20/20.

If you are experiencing some severe guilt that is hampering your ability to live a productive life, and you are unable to resolve it yourself, consider professional counseling. Most Christian counselors are well-experienced in helping their clients work through the useless emotions and condemnation of guilt.

9. Accept Your Understanding Of The Loss

You have probably asked, "Why?" over and over in your mind, and perhaps you have even reached a small degree of understanding. Use that as your viewpoint until you are able to work up to another level of understanding.

Just as time reduces the pain of a significant loss, it also increases your ability to understand the loss. In the Italian family which I mentioned earlier, their initial understanding of the sister's death was -- "God did not answer our prayers."

In time, however, they began to see that for almost three decades their sister smoked excessively, and it was the smoking of cigarettes, not God, that caused her to develop the fatal lung cancer.

10. Join A Group

Your old circle of friends may need to change. Even if it does not, you will need new friends for support. Friends who have been through a similar experience. Bereaved people sometimes form groups for friendship, support, and sharing.

11. Associate With Old Friends

This may be difficult at first. Some of your friends will be embarrassed by your presence and may not be sure how to act around you. They want to help. They value your friendship but are just not experienced in dealing with significant losses.

In time, they will learn how to interact with you if you give them a chance. You can help set the example by talking and acting as natural as possible and by not avoiding the subject of your loss.

12. Postpone Major Decisions!

This is one of the most vital guidelines I can give to you. Do not make any major decisions in your life for at least six months to a year.

For example, after any significant loss, wait at least six months before deciding to sell your home, divorce your spouse, or change jobs.

In the case of the Italian family I mentioned earlier, one of the most deeply bereaved sisters immediately divorced her husband ("life is too short") and started to live with another man. Now she is miserable.

No matter how deeply you "feel" about your current situation, make no major changes for at least six months.

13. Put Your Thoughts Into A Journal

If you are able to write, this process will help you get your feelings out and record your progress. Writing letters to say good-bye to your loved one can be painful, but the process is a helpful tool for many.

If you have lost a significant job, write down many of the good things you did on the job to remind yourself of the good work you performed. This will act to reinforce your worth to the working world.

Writing is a worthwhile form of grief relief and should be seriously considered as a means of helping you release your hurts.

14. Turn Grief Into Creative Energy

Find a way to help others. Helping to carry someone else's load is guaranteed to lighten your own load, for example:

If you have artistic ability, use it to teach the mentally handicapped in a local disability center.

> *Or...*

If you work with music, teach someone how to play your favorite musical instrument or if you like to read, find a blind person and read to them.

Seek productive and creative activities that are centered on "others". I am sure you understand the plan here.

God has designed us so that we are at our happiest when we often meet the needs of others. How many times have you heard someone say, "I am supposed to be helping them, but I am getting so much more out of it than they are!"

God has given each of us the need to assist others, and when we do, we are meeting our own, God-given needs. The Apostle Paul understood this principle well when he, writing in his letter to the church in Corinth, related his desire and ability to comfort others in the areas he had received comfort from the Lord (II Corinthians 1:3-7).

15. If Necessary, Do Not Hesitate To Get Professional Help.

Because this is the last thing mentioned on my list, I do not intend for you to think this is the last thing you should try. If you find that your grief is crippling your ability to function for a long period of time, seek professional help. Sometimes, just a few sessions with a trained counselor will help you to resolve the anger, guilt, and despair that keep you from functioning in the healthy manner which you did before your significant loss.

It is important to remember that no matter how deep your sorrow, you are not alone! Others have been there and will help share your load if you will allow them. You must not deny them the opportunity to minister to your need. As the Psalmist David said "this grief will pass", so also it will be with you. Your sorrow will pass.

In II Samuel chapter 12, David's son was very ill. David grieved many days before his son died. After the death of his son, he returned quickly to the responsibilities of his life saying, "I cannot bring him back, but I can go to him."

It was during this time of grief and sorrow that David wrote the Psalm that brings comfort to our hearts in moments such as these -- the twenty-third Psalm.
I have included the twenty-third Psalm in this book on a separate page. Let me suggest that you cut it out

and put it on your desk or on your night stand. As you read it, it will minister to your grieving heart.

You are loved, now let that love work for you in healing. Always remember, you are not alone. You have many friends, family, and Jesus Christ to minister to you and provide you with grief relief. Let them minister in love to your needs.

> *This time in your life will pass.*
> *You can and will make it through.*
> *Joy and hope will fill your life again.*
> *Let grief work its pain through.*
> *Remember, grief is the fruit of love.*

Stan E. DeKoven, Ph.D.

Chapter Ten

Caring For The Bereaved

As an elder, lay-counselor, pastor or Christian professional counselor, ministry to those suffering from loss is inevitable. In fact, we know that a major portion of many psychological disorders including: post-traumatic stress disorders, depression, adults molested as children, etc. are caused by the unresolved grief from significant loss. This section will attempt to provide some help for the Christian care giver and for each comforter who has been comforted by God, and is now in the position of helping others.

"Praise be to the God and Father of our Lord Jesus Christ, the Father of compassion and the God of all comfort, who comforts us in all our troubles, so that we can comfort those in any trouble with the comfort we ourselves have received from God.

For just as the sufferings of Christ flow over into our lives, so also through Christ our comfort overflows.

If we are distressed, it is for your comfort and salvation; if we are comforted, it is for your comfort, which produces in you patient endurance of the same sufferings we suffer.

And our hope for you is firm, because we know that just as you share in our sufferings, so also you share in our comfort" (2 Cor 1:3-7 NIV)

Paul's Admonition

The word "comfort" means to come alongside, to give care and nurture to one who is suffering. Paul admonishes all caregivers to practice the ministry of presence, of being with someone suffering from the pangs of grief and loss. It is more our caring presence that people need than our words (words will come in time). We need to use all our most empathetic listening skills to give care and support to the mourning man, woman or child.

Acknowledge and Affirm

Acknowledging the loss the person has experienced while affirming your compassionate care for the bereaved is an essential first step in the ministry process. The goals of grief counseling include:

1. To increase the reality of the loss. We increase the reality of loss by encouraging them to talk about their loss in present and eventually in past tense. This is a sensitive transition. It is human nature and a common response to try and hold on to the last object (Person circumstance or thing) by speaking of present and future relationships. As counselor we will slowly and with great sensitivity help them transition to a past tense orientation ("she was"...vs. "she is").

2. To assist the counselee to deal with the emotions, both present and past. The

sharing of emotion is healthy and appropriate. Yet, we cannot nor should we attempt to force what we think is an appropriate emotional reaction. We help provide an atmosphere of trust, and encourage their expression of healthy response. We must be prepared to help them face ambivalent (love, anger, fear, hope) reactions common to those experiencing grief.

3. To help the counselee overcome the impediment to readjustment. Through gentle questions and encouragement we lead them towards hope. Faith may wain, but hope in the goodness of God is our goal. We must somehow (not an easy task) help them to see beyond their loss to a future, unknown but negotiable.

4. To encourage the counselee to say an appropriate good-bye and to feel comfortable reinvesting back into life. (Warden, 1991). Saying goodbye is necessary before saying hello to life. I have accompanied many spouses to the graveyard to say a final farewell. Some will need help through role play, etc. However it is done, it is a goal, a process, which, like peeling an onion, may come layer by layer over time.

This process in counseling does not progress over-night. Essentially, the grief counseling process will go through stages similar to the grief relief stages. This will include processing through the denial, identifying and expressing the feelings related to the loss, providing of support for the continuance of life for the survivor, and facilitating the emotional relocation of the deceased loved one, through reminiscing, letting go, etc. During this time the counselor can help to interpret normal reactions and give support through the process.

When the grief process does not respond to these normal counseling techniques, the person may be experiencing complicated bereavement, which will necessitate a referral to a professionally trained therapist.

Beware of Anniversaries

The following excellent advice comes from Kay Cogswell, LCSW, the coordinator of Hospice of Grossmont Hospital in California. "Healing Through Grief", Sharp Healthcare, 1995.

"Being aware of how painful anniversaries can be, preparation for them and assistance through them is to be carefully planned and facilitated by a care giver.

The month before the anniversary is usually fraught with anxiety as we begin to dread the arrival of the actual day. Nightmares, insomnia and physical complaints are common, especially when we try to suppress the signs of acute grief (anger, despair, sadness, guilt, etc.) that tend to re-surge at this time. We often feel overwhelmed and confused by these anniversary reactions, questioning if we have made any progress in our griefwork at all.

Suggestions for Handling the Anniversary

1. Anticipate and prepare for the anniversary. When it comes to handling significant days (holidays, birthdays, etc.) it is better to anticipate the difficulty and plan how you want to spend the day rather than try to ignore it.

2. Accept the fact that the time before and immediately after the anniversary will be painful. The actual anniversary date is rarely as devastating as we actually anticipated.

3. Find a way to acknowledge the significance of the day and to remember the person who has died.

   • Have a religious service dedicated to the person who has died.
   • Have flowers significantly placed in memory of the person who has died.
   • Plan a special anniversary ritual. You can do this alone or with family members and friends.

4. Do something fun that you did or planned to do with your loved one.

5. Use your journal.

6. Indulge and nurture yourself. In the days around the anniversary be gentle with yourself. Limit your expectations and responsibilities. Engage the coping strategies and nurturing

activities which you have found valuable throughout your grief process.

Everyone will experience loss in their own unique way. As a care-giver, you need to be just that -- a giver of care in the name of Jesus. All of us as members of the Body of Christ (the Church) are admonished to give care to others, as we pass through the valley. Let us remember the words of the Psalmist David.

PSALM 23

A Psalm of David. The LORD is my shepherd; I shall not want.

He maketh me to lie down in green pastures: he leadeth me beside the still waters.

He restoreth my soul: he leadeth me in the paths of righteousness for his name's sake.

Yea, though I walk through the valley of the shadow of death, I will fear no evil: for thou art with me; thy rod and thy staff they comfort me.

Thou preparest a table before me in the presence of mine enemies: thou anointest my head with oil; my cup runneth over.

Surely goodness and mercy shall follow me all the days of my life: and I will dwell in the house of the LORD for ever.

Stan E. DeKoven, Ph.D.

Epilogue

On January 24th 2000, my bride of 26 years, Karen, passed away. She had suffered under the ravages of brain cancer. My daughters, family and friends world wide suffered with us. Karen fought hard, she wanted to live, we went through the roller coaster of hope and despair, and on the morning of January 24th 2000 she died in faith.

My shock was profound, the sense of relief at the ending of Karen's suffering was overwhelming, but to my surprise, there was joy. Not joy in the death, for death from our view is an ugly thing. But after discovering that she was gone to be with the Father, an inner joy expressed in a spontaneous song rose up within me. I cannot remember nor explain the song but am grateful that the Holy Spirit provided such tangible comfort in the midst of my despair.

Later that evening, after robotically taking care of Karen's funeral arrangements and making numerous phone calls I attempted to sleep. It was fitful at best. Somewhere around two in the morning as I woke with a start, I heard from the Lord deep in my heart that he had a word for me and for the body of Christ. I was led to Hebrews 12:1-14. God spoke that in this passage I would find keys to finding the courage to survive a crisis of immense proportions. May it speak to you.

"Therefore, since we have so great a cloud of witnesses surrounding us, let us also lay aside every encumbrance and the sin which so easily entangles us, and let us run with endurance the race that is set before us, fixing our eyes

on Jesus, the author and perfecter of faith, who for the joy set before Him endured the cross, despising the shame, and has sat down at the right hand of the throne of God.

For consider Him who has endured such hostility by sinners against Himself, so that you will not grow weary and lose heart.

You have not yet resisted to the point of shedding blood in your striving against sin; and you have forgotten the exhortation which is addressed to you as sons, 'My son, do not regard lightly the discipline of the lord, nor faint when you are reproved by him; for those whom the lord loves He disciplines, and He scourges every son whom He receives." It is for discipline that you endure; God deals with you as with sons; for what son is there whom his father does not discipline?

But if you are without discipline, of which all have become partakers, then you are illegitimate children and not sons. Furthermore, we had earthly fathers to discipline us, and we respected them; shall we not much rather be subject to the Father of spirits, and live?

For they disciplined us for a short time as seemed best to them, but He disciplines us for our good, so that we may share His holiness.

All discipline for the moment seems not to be joyful, but sorrowful; yet to those who have been trained by it, afterwards it yields the peaceful fruit of righteousness. Therefore, strengthen the hands that are weak and the knees that are feeble, and make straight paths for your feet, so that the limb which is lame may not be put out of joint, but rather be healed.

Pursue peace with all men, and the sanctification without which no one will see the Lord. (NASB)

Here are the seven points God gave me when hope was gone, in the middle of shock and despair, at my lowest moment...God.

1. We... all have a journey, a purpose to fulfill. Joseph had his purpose, but a pit, Potiphar's wife, prison and Pharaoh had to be traversed before he saw the fulfillment of his purpose. Paul had this heavenly vision, Stephen saw heaven, all died having fulfilled their purpose. Thus whether our journey is short or long, God is the Lord of the journey.

2. We... are not alone in our journey. Even in our worst days, God will provide us with good comforters, friends to listen, and fellow travelers. We need them. We must journey with them.

3. We... have a waymaker; author and perfecter. Phil 1:6 became a personal promise and comfort for me in regard to Karen. It states "I am confident in this very thing, that he who began a good work in you will perfect it until the day of Christ Jesus." Whatever the full purpose of Karen's life, I know she fulfilled it...because I know.

4. We... know struggles will come, pain and loss may (probably) be our experience but ultimately, as we trust in Christ there is joy. Karen's illness and death were hell for me and my family...we were not exempt...no one is. Why did Karen die...she contracted a deadly,

incurable cancer. All of us will face crisis. We must trust God in spite of our circumstances, for we know he is faithful.

5. We... have a responsibility in our daily walk, which includes laying aside weights and sins, so we can complete our course. Grieving is necessary, mourning is healthy. None of us can carry the weight of grief alone, nor the sense of woundedness from our loss. Somehow with God's help we must lay it aside. Easier said than done...a necessary process. Further, we must recognize that, as unfair as it may seem, if we are still alive, we are to run our race, live our life, for the long haul. Why Karen? Why not me? All normal questions without satisfactory (psychological) answers. God is sovereign... but we still do not understand. Yet, if we keep our eyes on Jesus, we can find renewed purpose for our lives, especially as we consider all Christ has done for us.

6. We... are to finish strong, which requires discipline. Discipline does not mean punishment. Though we might feel as though God is punishing us through our loss, this is certainly not true. God is love...and all circumstances we face will work out for good to those who love God and are called according to his purpose (Rom 8:28). Finishing strong, coming to acceptance, requires acknowledging our:

   a. Sonship... we are inheritors of the grace of God. We are part of God's family. That family has two locations...here and in heaven. Karen will not come to me, but I will go to her in God's time. In the meantime, I must recognize my responsibility to act as a son (mature, equipped and prepared).

b. Love from the Father...which is sure

c. Submission to God's sovereignty, for God's ways are not ours, yet we know that "precious in the eyes of the Lord is the death of his saints (Psalm 116:15). I may never fully understand this yet I know, I know.

7. We... receive kingdom life, as we avoid a root of bitterness which can ruin us. We all have a choice, as we grieve, with God's help and much support to embrace God's Kingdom benefits, righteousness, peace and joy in the Holy Ghost (Rom 14:17) or we can reject God's love grace and mercy, become bitter and refuse to grow.

A Wonderful Conclusion

A number months after Cynthia's husbands' death (who we met briefly in the beginning of this book) she met a man who came to her church. They had polite initial meetings, with no initial connection, but eventually developed a positive friendship.

A few months later they started dating and God began to knit their hearts together. Four years previously she had lost her husband to premature death. Now, in the wonderful mercy of God, Bill Jefferies became Cynthia's husband. They love each other, will continue to love and miss their former spouses, but rejoice in God's answer to prayer for them.

Of course, not all stories will end as well. In fact, none of us knows if we or a loved one will have to experience the walk through the dark shadow of death. Thus, it is essential that we chose to embrace life and risk an uncertain future. For God is good, grief is for a season, weeping is for the night, but in the morning...joy!

Bibliography

Bohac, Joseph J. Human Development: A Christian Perspective. Ramona: Vision Publishing. 1993.

Bolby, J. *Separation Anxiety.* International Journal Psychoanalysis.

Callahan, Maggie. & Kelley, Patricia. Final Gifts. New York: Bantam Books. 1992.

Coombs, Don C. Grief Work. Southgate, MI. 1995

Graham, Billy. Facing Death -- And the Life After. Waco: Word Books. 1987.

Greaves, Helen. Testimony of Light. London: Latimer Trend & Company. 1969.

Levine, Stephen. Healing Into Life and Death. New York: 1987.

Lifton, Robert Jay. The Broken Connection. New York: Simon and Schuster. 1979.

Linn, Matthew, Fabricant, Sheila, and Linn, Dennis. Healing the Eight Stages of Life. Mahwah: Paulist Press. 1988.

Mahler, M. S. The Psychological Birth of the Human Infant. New York: Basic Books. 1975.

Morey, Robert A. Death and the Afterlife. Minneapolis: Bethany House Publishers. 1984.

Morrell, David. Fireflies. New York: E.P. Dutton. 1988.

Owen, Virginia S. "The Dark Side of Grace." *Christianity Today*. (July 19, 1993). Pp. 32-35.

Ross-Kubler, Elisabeth. On Death and Dying. New York: Macmillian Publishing. 1969. Cliffs: Prentice-Hall, Inc. 1975.

Simmel, M.L. "A study of phantoms after amputation of the breast." Neuropsychology. 1966.

Spiegel, Youch. The Grief Process: Analysis and Counseling. Nashville: Abington Press. 1977.

Sudnow, David. Passing On. Englewood Cliffs: Prentice-Hall, Inc. 1967.

Warden, William. Grief Counseling and Grief Therapy. New York: Springer Publishing. 1991.

Zinker, Joseph C. Rosa Lee: Motivation and the Crisis of Dying. Painesville: The Lake Erie College Press. 1966.

The Holy Bible. Grand Rapids: Zondervan Bible Publishers. 1973.

The Teaching Ministry of Dr. Stan DeKoven

Dr. Stan DeKoven conducts seminars and professional workshops, both nationally and internationally, based on his books and extensive experience in Practical Christian Living. He is available for limited engagements at Church Seminars, retreats and conferences. For a complete listing of topics and books, we invite you to contact:

Dr. Stan DeKoven, President
Vision International College and University
1115 D Street
Ramona, CA. 92065
760-789-4700 (in California) or
1-800-9 VISION
Email: sdekoven@vision.edu
www.vision.edu

Other Helpful Books by Dr. DeKoven on related topics include:

- *On Belay! Introduction to Christian Counseling*
- *Journey to Wholeness: Restoration of the Soul (Living According to the Patterns of God)*
- *Family Violence: Patterns of Destruction*
- *Crisis Counseling*
- *Forty Days to the Promise: A Way Through the Wilderness*
- *Marriage and Family Life: A Christian Perspective*
- *I Want to Be Like You, Dad: Breaking Free from Generational Patterns-Restoring the Heart of the Father*
- *Parenting on Purpose*

Stan E. DeKoven, Ph.D.

CPSIA information can be obtained at www.ICGtesting.com
Printed in the USA
BVOW040934150313

315486BV00003B/3/A